QUICK AND
COLORFUL
Appliqué

QUICK AND COLORFUL

Appliqué

14 Lively New Designs

EDITED BY
ROSEMARY WILKINSON

Martingale®
& COMPANY

First published in 2006 by New Holland Publishers (UK) Ltd
London | Cape Town | Sydney | Auckland
www.newhollandpublishers.com
Garfield House, 86–88 Edgware Road, London W2 2EA
80 McKenzie Street, Cape Town 8001, South Africa
Unit 4, 14 Aquatic Drive, Frenchs Forest, NSW 2086, Australia
218 Lake Road, Northcote, Auckland, New Zealand

That Patchwork Place® is an imprint of Martingale & Company®.
Martingale & Company
20205 144th Ave. NE
Woodinville, WA 98072-8478 USA
www.martingale-pub.com

Library of Congress Cataloging-in-Publication data is available.
ISBN: 1-56477-682-4

MISSION STATEMENT
Dedicated to providing quality products
and service to inspire creativity.

Editor: Rosemary Wilkinson
Design: Frances de Rees
Photographs: Shona Wood
Illustrations: Carrie Hill
Template diagrams: Stephen Dew

Reproduction by Pica Digital PTE Ltd, Singapore
Printed and bound in Malaysia by Times Offset (M) Sdn Bhd

11 10 09 08 07 06   8 7 6 5 4 3 2 1

CONTENTS

Getting Started

Types of fabric to use for patchwork and appliqué

The most popular type of fabric for patchwork and the easiest to work with is 100% cotton. Fabric designers produce coordinating ranges of patterns specifically for patchwork, using a common color palette, so that all the designs will work together. These fabrics are very good quality and can be purchased from your local quilt shop or online sources. If you are going to spend time and money making a quilt, it's nice to know that you are working with good-quality materials, so that the quilt will last for a long time.

Cotton is also very suitable for hand-stitched appliqué, because it can be folded and manipulated and a crisp edge can be obtained, even when working with quite small pieces. It's also suitable for fusible appliqué.

Manufacturers have recently started to introduce different fabrics, such as silk and damask, that coordinate with their cotton fabrics for us to experiment with, which is an exciting development.

Some fabrics, such as poly-cottons, are really too "bouncy" to enable the quilter to achieve a crisp finish when the fabrics are folded and stitched. As you become more experienced, you will become aware of how different fabrics perform.

A good rule to follow for a professional finish is to make sure that all the fabrics in the quilt are the same weight and thickness. However, there are exceptions to the rule, such as crazy patchwork, a traditional Victorian technique. Contemporary art quilts also break the rules, where paper, plastic, and other unusual fabrics are used.

Another important factor to consider when buying fabric is the size and direction of the pattern. Bold designs can sometimes be too big for small patches, although this can work to your advantage if the pieces are cut carefully. Some fabrics have a very obvious one-way design, which can cause a problem when cutting small pieces; however, they can be very effective when used in borders.

Fabric preparation

Many quilters prefer to wash all their fabrics before using them, and there are two reasons why. First, cotton shrinks when washed, so it's better to take care of this before piecing. Second, washing dark fabrics helps get rid of any excess dye.

General equipment

Anyone with a basic sewing kit at home could take up patchwork by hand. However if you wish to piece your quilt by machine, there are some basic tools you will need to invest in. Designed for speed and accuracy, these tools go hand-in-hand with your sewing machine and will enhance your sewing. Sewing machines vary from those offering a basic straight stitch to those with a wide range of decorative stitches. The choice largely depends on your price range, although a machine with a zigzag stitch is a requirement for machine-appliqué work.

The three most essential tools are a rotary cutter, a self-healing cutting mat printed with measurements, and an acrylic ruler. These all come in different sizes, but as a basic guide, a 45 mm cutter, a medium-sized cutting mat, and a ruler long enough to span the mat should get you started (diagram 1).

Rotary cutter: The cutter is capable of cutting through several layers of fabric at a time and for this reason it is extremely sharp. It will have a guard to cover the blade when not in use.

Please train yourself to put the guard on whenever you are not actually using it. Also keep it in a safe place away from children and pets.

Avoid rolling your cutter over a pin or other solid object because this will ruin the blade by giving it a dull spot. If you

diagram 1

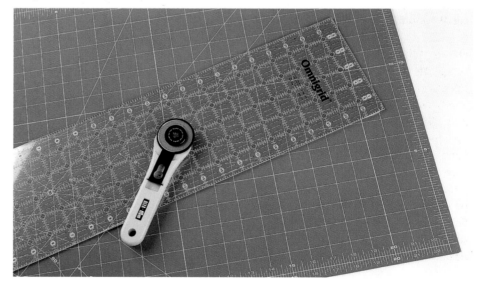

have not used a cutter before, try practicing on old sheets or scrap fabrics before cutting new fabric. Eventually you will have to replace the blade, though, due to normal wear and tear. Keep the case from the new blade and use it to dispose of the old one safely.

Self-healing cutting mat: Usually green or gray in color, these are available with either metric or imperial measurements. After you make a cut with the rotary cutter, the cut line closes up again, so that the mat can be used repeatedly. Cutting mats come in a range of sizes. The biggest ones make cutting strips easiest, but a smaller size is more portable.

Note

Keep the mat flat and away from sources of heat, such as radiators, because it will be useless if warped.

Ruler: Eventually you will probably buy several different rulers, because different sizes are suitable for different jobs. A square ruler can be useful when working with blocks, and square rulers also come in different sizes. Every ruler should have accurate measurements marked on it, and also may have guidelines to help you cut 45° and 60° angles.

Other items you will need

Template plastic: This is used to make templates for appliqué and patchwork, and is available from quilting shops.

Pins: Flower-head pins are best because they lie flat, but they can be expensive.

Pencils: Pencils with sharp points (disposable mechanical pencils are good) are good for marking fabric. Silver or yellow pencils are handy for dark fabrics.

Scissors: I recommend a dressmaking size and a craft size; a smaller embroidery size could be very useful for smaller work.

You will also need scissors which can be used just for paper. Paper will blunt your fabric scissors, which need to be kept nice and sharp.

Needles: A selection of sizes is useful, plus "quilting/betweens" are needed for hand quilting. Buy size 8 or 9 to start with and progress to size 10 as your hand quilting improves. The higher the number, the smaller the needle.

Sewing-machine needles: Refer to your sewing-machine manual for information on which needle to use and always keep a spare packet with your machine. Specialty needles are available, such as for machine quilting (finer) and for metallic thread (large eye with a groove in the side of the needle).

Safety pins: You can buy special quilters' safety pins which are slightly curved on the bottom to enable you to pin the three layers of the quilt together. If you have to move the quilt about, they stay in place better than straight pins, which tend to wriggle their way out.

Hand quilting supplies

Thimbles, or finger protection: these are used to protect the fingers during hand quilting, which involves pushing the needle through the layers of fabric and batting to form tiny running stitches. In one quilt there will be thousands of these stitches and you would find that without protection, the skin of your quilting fingers would quickly become sore. For this reason there are various types of thimbles and finger protectors on the market. It is a matter of personal choice (and a certain amount of trial and error) which you prefer to work with.

Quilting hoop: If you are going to be doing a lot of quilting, you may wish to buy a quilting hoop. These are either wooden or plastic and range in sizes. A 12"- or 14"-diameter hoop is a good choice. Bind the hoops with white cotton tape to prevent damaging the fabric of the quilt.

Appliqué supplies

Freezer paper: This is used for making templates which can be adhered to the fabric with an iron.

Small appliqué pins: These tiny pins help hold the appliqué pieces in place until they are stitched down.

A pin board: A portable board onto which you can pin small pieces will help keep everything in place until needed.

Rotary cutting

Practice on old sheets or unwanted fabric and don't try to cut through too many layers at first. Remove any clutter from your workspace and have all your equipment within easy reach. Make sure the work table is a comfortable height.

1 Take your fabric to the cutting mat and fold it in half, wrong sides together, with selvages aligned at the top and the cut edge facing toward your cutting hand. Ideally, the mat should be big enough to fit the full width of the folded fabric. Before cutting any pieces, you need to ensure that the cut edge of the fabric is straight and at a right angle to the selvages. Cutting accuracy depends on this. It will also help you to establish a straight grain of fabric. Place the ruler on the fabric close to the cut edge, aligning one of the horizontal lines on the ruler with the fold of the fabric. If the cut edge is not exactly parallel to one of the vertical lines on the ruler, cut off a small strip to straighten the edge (diagram 2).

diagram 2

2 Carefully turn the straight edge of the fabric to face in the opposite direction. Now you will be using the ruler as a tool to cut accurate pieces. Cutting instructions in a quilt pattern usually start with asking you to cut a strip, then to turn the strip and cut off smaller pieces, either squares or rectangles. For example, if you need 4" squares, first cut a 4"-wide strip from your fabric, as follows. Lay the fabric on the mat with the straight edge of the fabric to the left (or right if you are left-handed). Line up the 4" line of the ruler against the edge of your fabric. The area now trapped under the ruler will be a 4"-wide strip. Double-check this by counting on your ruler from right to left. Now press down firmly on the ruler with your left (or non-cutting) hand, take the rotary cutter in the other hand, line the blade up against the ruler just below the fabric and, pushing away from you, cut along the length of the ruler going from bottom to top (diagram 3). Be sure to always cut away from yourself to prevent a cutting injury!

diagram 3

3 Turn the strip of fabric so that it is lying sideways across the board and trim off the selvages. You can now cut this in the same way to form a 4" square. Remember to work from the left, trap the required amount of fabric under the ruler (by lining up with the 4" line on the ruler), double-check, and then cut from bottom to top. This produces two square because the fabric is folded.

Repeat this until you have the required amount of squares (diagram 4). This is known as crosscutting.

diagram 4

The cutting instructions in the projects that follow will specify the width of the strips you'll need to cut across the width of the fabric, as well as the specific pieces you'll need to crosscut. They assume the rotary-cutting method described above will be used.

You can cut strips, rectangles and triangles using this method, you just need to be organized and be able to count!

Chain piecing
If you have identical pairs of shapes to be sewn together, you can save time and thread by taking them to the machine and stitching continuously across the pieces until all the pieces are sewn together (diagram 5). You can then cut the thread between the pairs and press the individual pieces—often referred to as "units." This method can be used for triangles, squares, and rectangles.

diagram 5

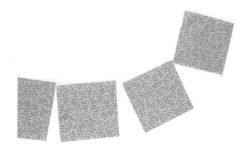

Quick-pieced triangles
There are many more tried and tested methods to speed up your patchwork. The method described below is very successful if you are making lots of squares made up of two triangles (called "half-square triangles") and also works well with chain piecing.

If you want to end up with a particular-sized pieced square, you will need to add ⅞" to the finished size to obtain the cut size. For instance, if you want two half-square triangles to end up as a 4" square, you must cut the original squares ⅞" bigger, or 4⅞". If you use this calculation every time you want to make half-square triangles using the following method, then you can't go wrong. (Note that this is ⅜" more than the standard ½" added to the finished size of a plain square for seam allowances, which equals ¼" per side.)

1 Take two different squares of the required size and color to the cutting board. Place them right sides together, with the lighter one on top. With a ruler and sharp-pointed pencil, draw a diagonal line across the square from corner to corner, repeating on the remaining pairs of squares (diagram 6).

diagram 6

2 Machine stitch ¼" to the left of the diagonal line on the first pair of squares, then chain piece all the remaining squares in this way. When complete, turn the chain around and start stitching from the other end, ¼" away from the opposite side of the diagonal line in the same way (diagram 7).

diagram 7

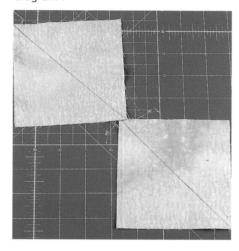

3 Cut the pieces apart. Take one set of squares to the cutting mat and cut along the marked diagonal line. Open, press, and you will have two squares made up of two triangles each (diagram 8). Repeat for all the squares.

diagram 8

Appliqué

Appliqué is the process of attaching pieces of fabric to a background fabric. There are quite a few ways which you can successfully apply one fabric to another, creating a pattern or even a new surface. Here we'll review both hand and machine appliqué.

Hand appliqué

There are a few different ways of doing hand appliqué. The freezer-paper method, which is an easy one to start with, is described first.

Freezer-paper method

Freezer paper, found in the food-wrap aisle of grocery stores or in some quilt shops, is handy for appliqué. It is shiny on one side and dull or matte on the other. The shiny side can be ironed onto the fabric, lifted and repositioned, time after time. Alternatively, it can be left in place as a template for forming the appliqué shape, as in this method.

If you cannot obtain freezer paper, you can do this with ordinary printer paper, but it will not have the advantage of sticking to the fabric. You'll need to pin plain paper in place.

1 A simple heart is the perfect shape for learning how to appliqué because itprovides curves, straight edges, and inner and outer points to stitch. Place a piece of freezer paper, shiny side down, over the heart pattern and trace the heart onto the dull side of the paper (diagram 9).

diagram 9

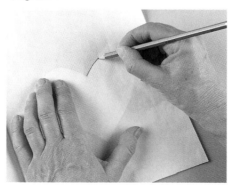

2 Cut out the freezer-paper shape exactly on the marked line to make a template and iron it to the wrong side of the fabric, which should be at least ¼" bigger all the way around than the paper shape. Trim the seam allowance to a scant ¼" (diagram 10).

diagram 10

3 Leaving the freezer paper in place, pin the shape to the background fabric using appliqué pins. Thread a needle with thread to match the appliqué shape, bring the needle to the front of the fabric, then use the tip to turn under ¼" of the appliqué fabric. You will be able to feel the freezer paper inside, and you can use it as an edge against which to turn the fabric, creating a crisp fold. Take a tiny appliqué stitch (like a slip stitch) on the fold of the material, from the front to the back of the work, to stitch down the turned edge (diagram 11).

diagram 11

Continue stitching around the heart, stopping about 1" from the beginning. Take the freezer paper out and stitch up the gap.

Paper template

Another method is to make a paper template of the desired shape and draw around it on the right side of the fabric.

1 Cut out the fabric ¼" outside the marked line, then place the fabric shape over the paper template, fold over the seam allowance, and loosely tack in place (diagram 12).

diagram 12

2 Pin this piece to the background fabric and stitch using a tiny appliqué stitch as before (diagram 13). The paper can either be left in place permanently or can be removed through a tiny incision from the reverse side of the background fabric.

diagram 13

Interfacing

A third method is to cut out your shape in the chosen fabric, including a ¼" seam allowance, then cut a piece of interfacing roughly the same size. Place the interfacing on the right side of the fabric and stitch the two together using a ¼" seam allowance and leaving a small gap to turn the shape inside out (diagram 14). Trim the interfacing even with the fabric shape.

diagram 14

You will find that you have a neat edge which you can then stitch to the background, with the added advantage that you do not have to turn the edges as you stitch (diagram 15).

diagram 15

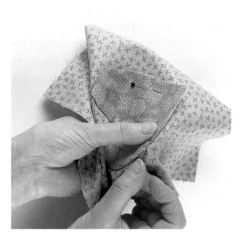

If you are working with sharp curves and intricate shapes you may find it necessary to clip the seam allowance slightly, to allow the fabric to "give" more.

Fusible appliqué

In this method, the pieces are applied to the background fabric using fusible web. This is usually finished by machine stitching around the raw edge (satin stitch, open zigzag or blanket stitch), but the stitching can also be done by hand (blanket stitch). Fusible web is very thin fabric glue attached to a sheet of transparent paper. Initially it will be rough on one side (the glue side) and smooth on the other. (You can trace onto this side.)

1 Make a plastic template of the shape that you wish to appliqué to your fabric. Trace the shape onto the smooth side of the fusible web. Cut out roughly about ¼" outside the marked line (diagram 16).

diagram 16

2 Place the fabric for the appliqué wrong side up on the work surface and put the fusible-web shape, rough side down, on top. Iron in place. Now cut the shape out exactly on the marked line (diagram 17).

diagram 17

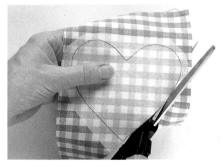

3 Peel off the paper backing, leaving the glue on the fabric. Position the shape where you want it, glue side down, on the right side of the background fabric and carefully iron it to bond the two fabrics together (diagram 18). This will now stay in place until it is stitched.

diagram 18

4 Stitch in place with a satin or zigzag stitch. The ideal is to just cover the edge of the shape without stitching too much into the background fabric (diagram 19). Stitch slowly to make smooth curves.

diagram 19

You can cut out some very tiny, intricate shapes with this method, but remember that by tracing on to the backing paper, your shape will be **reversed** when you finally iron it in place. If you don't want a mirror image, you must trace the image on tracing paper, reverse it, and trace again onto the fusible web.

Hints and tips for appliqué by machine

These hints and tips apply to satin stitch as well as to blanket stitch or an open zigzag stitch.

● I always recommend that you practice first if you have not done machine appliqué before. First set your machine to a satin stitch and do a sample.

● Every machine varies slightly, so it is important that you make a note of any stitch settings (width and length) that you find work well. (You should be able to vary the density of the cover of the satin stitch by altering the stitch length and width.) If you practice on muslin, you can write the information directly on the muslin sample.

● You may also find it useful to make a note of thread type, needle size, etc. If you file these, you will build up a good portfolio of samples for later reference.

● Start with the needle down in the fabric so that you'll know exactly where you are starting. If the appliqué shape has a gentle curve, you should be able to maneuver the needle around the shape as you stitch.

● If you are working with geometric or angular shapes, you will need to stop at each sharp corner with the needle down in the work, lift up the presser foot, turn the fabric, put down the presser foot, and start stitching again.

● Plan your work so that you change the thread color as little as possible. On a project this could mean appliquéing all the blue pieces first, then the red, and so on.

Raw-edge appliqué

Mainly used in contemporary quilts, this type of appliqué can be done with or without fusible web, but if done without, use pins to anchor the appliqué while it is being stitched.

1 Cut the fabric shape out to the exact size you want (do not add a seam allowance), then pin, baste, or fabric glue in place.

2 To anchor the shape to the background, you can use a variety of threads and hand or machine stitches, which may be decorative or functional (diagram 20). With time this kind of work will probably fray a little, but depending on your quilt style, this can be acceptable.

diagram 20

Couching

Particularly useful for adding surface decoration to your quilt, couching refers to the placement of threads or thin strips of fabric onto the quilt surface, then stitching them in place by hand or machine—usually with decorative stitches. Any stitch on the machine that involves the needle swinging from side to side, such as the zigzag, can be used.

Batting

To be a quilt, your work must officially have three layers: a top (which may be pieced), backing fabric, and batting sandwiched in between.

The three most popular types of batting are 100% polyester, which comes in a variety of thicknesses; 100% cotton; and a blend of 80% cotton/20% polyester. Normally batting is white (bleached) or natural (unbleached). Black or dark gray polyester batting is available too; if you are making a black or very dark quilt, it would be advisable to use this.

Within these fiber-content categories there are many variations, and by the time you have made two or three quilts, you will find a favorite. Silk and wool batting are also available, but they are more expensive and not as common. Silk drapes beautifully and wool re-creates the quilts of old because it shrinks when washed, giving a wrinkled appearance to the quilt. Cotton batting also shrinks, is sometimes pre-washed, and usually comes with some information about this, so check before you buy. One more type of batting worth mentioning is thermal, which is useful for making place mats, table runners, and similar items. It lies very flat. You may consider using fleece (the type fleece jackets are made of) on the back of a quilt, as in "Promenade Throw" on page 64. Projects using fleece don't need batting, but I would not recommend using fleece for a large project.

You may hear "loft" mentioned in reference to batting. This is the thickness of the batting, which will affect the depth of the quilted effect.

Another term you may come across is "bearding." This is the amount of little batting fibers which come through the fabric when you are quilting. This is the reason you may wish to use black batting for darker projects.

Your choice of batting may also be affected by the person who will be using the quilt. For babies, natural fibers are recommended, but if you're making a playmat or picnic mat which would need constant washing, you would probably choose polyester for its durability.

Batting comes in various widths, and quilt shops generally stock a variety of styles on rolls. It also comes packaged in sizes suitable for different beds, from cribs to king size.

Batting suitable for appliqué

Before deciding which batting to use for appliqué projects, you should decide what type of quilting you are going to use. For hand quilting, you should choose one of the softer types of batting that will be easy to stitch through, which means it will also be easier on your hands. The best choices are probably polyester or a very thin, soft cotton.

Batting left to right: silk, cotton, 2 oz cream polyester, black cotton, 80%/20% cotton/polyester, wool, gray polyester, white polyester

For machine quilting, you have a much wider choice because it is the machine that is going to be doing the stitching.

Take advice from the package recommendations as to how close together the quilting lines should be, such as 4", 6", or 8". Normally, appliquéd projects will have outline quilting around the appliqué shapes, so they may be quite densely quilted in some cases. If in doubt, I would always recommend that you try making a sample with a small quilt sandwich.

Making the quilt sandwich

As mentioned earlier, a quilt has three layers. In order to achieve a good finish, you must first put the layers together carefully, keeping them as flat and wrinkle free as possible before starting to quilt.

Ideally you should buy the backing and batting so that they are slightly larger than the quilt top—about 3" all around. The extra batting and backing fabric will be trimmed after the quilting is finished.

1 Tape the quilt backing right side down to a large table or to the floor.

2 Center the batting on top of this.

3 Finally add your ironed quilt top right side up.

4 Pin the layers together, keeping them as flat and smooth as possible. Start pinning your quilt from the center outward (diagram 21).

diagram 21

5 Basting can now start. Using white thread and a large needle, and always working from the center outward, baste through all three layers in a grid of lines approximately 4" to 6" apart (diagram 22). I cannot stress how important this step is if you want to achieve good quilting results. It is just not worth cutting corners; even if it seems a little tedious, basting will be well worth it in the end.

diagram 22

The "sandwich" is now ready to be quilted. Your quilt top will come to life once it is quilted due to all the texture that the stitches create. Again you have choices as to the quilting method. Some people will enjoy hand quilting, more than machine quilting, and vice versa. And some people do both.

Transferring quilting designs

One frequently asked question is how to transfer a quilting design onto your quilt or, indeed, what type of quilting to use.

Transfer the design onto the quilt before layering and basting. Stencils make it easy to mark a design onto a quilt top. Use an air- or water-soluble pen for marks that are easy to remove. For dark fabrics, a silver or yellow pencil will make the marks easier to see, and these pencils sometimes come with an eraser, or the marks just wear off in time. Another option for marking a stenciled design is to use an ordinary lead pencil.

Another method is to draw the design onto tissue paper and then baste it to the quilt. You can machine stitch over the paper and then tear it away afterward.

For the design itself there are many choices. Basically, a geometric quilt will call for geometric style quilting, and an abstract quilt might call for more abstract, random quilting—unless you want to break all the rules!

Machine quilting

You can do all of the above-mentioned quilting styles with machine quilting. Machine quilting will appear as a continuous line of stitching on the surface of the quilt, unlike hand quilting which has broken lines. However, some modern machines have a feature that makes the stitching look like a broken line.

For machine quilting, you will need a walking foot. Consult your sewing machine supplier (have make and model number handy) so that you get the right one. The object of the walking foot is to feed the layers of the quilt evenly over the feed dogs of your machine as you quilt. If you were to use an ordinary presser foot, it would apply too much pressure to the backing fabric, giving you major problems (and puckers) in your quilt.

If you want to do free-motion machine quilting, you will also need a darning or embroidery foot, and you need to be able to drop the feed dogs of your machine

Always start quilting in the center of the quilt. If it is a large quilt, you will probably need to roll it up in order to do this. Try not to let the weight of the quilt drag on the needle because this will affect the quality of the stitching. Practice makes perfect, and it is probably best if you start with a small project and work up.

Whatever type of quilting you decide to do, there will always be thread ends to deal with. These should be sewn securely into the middle layer of the quilt so that they cannot ever come unraveled. Try "easy threading" needles if you only have very short ends of thread left. These have a slot in the top of the needle for easy threading.

Quilting in the ditch

With this method, the stitches aren't always visible, but they help emphasize the patchwork or appliqué shapes. Using the walking foot, stitch along a seam line by slightly parting where the seam lies, and then letting it settle back after stitching (diagram 23). The loft of the batting helps to disguise the quilting.

diagram 23

Echo or outline quilting

This is a term used to describe quilting ¼" away from the shape or seam line (diagram 24).

diagram 24

Free-motion machine quilting

If you are a beginner, you may find it easier to start with quilting in the ditch before moving on to free-motion machine quilting. This method is also described as "taking the needle for a walk"—you will see why when you give it a try. As mentioned above, you will need a darning or embroidery foot and to drop the feed dogs on the sewing machine for this type of quilting (refer to the manufacturer's handbook if in doubt).

The most popular type of free-motion machine quilting is stippling, which looks like vermicelli. It's a meandering pattern where the paths of the stitching do not cross (diagram 25). The beauty of this is that it can be done large or small, and you can cover large open spaces on quilts with it. Experiment with different patterns. Basically, if you can draw it with a pencil, then you can quilt it.

diagram 25

Other types of patterns you can free-motion stitch include loops, spirals, feathers, flowers, butterflies, shells, and many more.

Hand quilting

Just as with machine quilting, it takes a lot of practice to become good at hand quilting.

You will need a quilting hoop and thimbles (see page 7). The design needs to be marked on the quilt top before the quilt is placed in the hoop (see page 13). Unlike embroidery, the quilt needs to be slack in the hoop. Hand quilting needles are tiny (see page 7). The stitches look like running stitches on the surface, but are done in such a way that the back is identical to the front. Make sure you are sitting comfortably before you start, and that you have good light. Always start in the center of the quilt and work outward.

1 Thread your needle with one of the good quality hand-quilting threads available. (Some are waxed to aid quilting.) Knot the end. From the back of the work (underneath the fabric contained in the hoop), come up through the layers of the quilt sandwich with the needle. To hide the knot in the batting layer, gently tug on the thread to "pop" it through the backing fabric.

2 Now the needle should be on the top side of the work. You should be able to see your pattern clearly. Push the needle and thread straight down until you feel the receiving finger, which should be ready underneath; place your thumb slightly ahead of the first stitch to act as a tension guide (diagram 26).

diagram 26

3 Guide the needle back up to the surface by almost bouncing off the underneath thimble. Repeat this, eventually achieving several stitches on the needle at once. This has sometimes been described as a "rocking" action. At first this will seem awkward, but if you practice regularly you will be able to load the needle with a number of stitches before pulling the thread through the layers.
Note: Take the quilt out of the hoop in between working sessions so the hoop doesn't crease the fabric.

Big-stitch quilting

A modern version of traditional hand quilting, big-stitch quilting has evolved along with art quilts and contemporary work, and is a crossover between embroidery and quilting. Threads such as pearl cotton and embroidery floss can be used to both quilt and embellish at the same time. As the name suggests, the stitches are larger than normal, but still fairly even in size (diagram 27). A chenille needle is helpful for this technique because it is sharp with a big eye for thick threads to pass through. Other stitches, such as cross-stitch, herringbone and feather stitch, could also be used.

diagram 27

Binding the quilt

Once the quilting is finished, remove all basting; then you will need to bind the edges of your quilt. This can be done in a fabric of your choice, but it is often darker than the other fabrics because binding acts as a frame around the quilt.

Continuous double-fold method

For this method, binding strips are cut across the width of the fabric and joined together in one long strip with diagonal seams before being sewn to the quilt layers.

1 Place the ends of two binding strips right sides together so that they are

perpendicular to one another (forming an L shape). Sew the strips together so that the seam runs diagonally from one outside corner to the other. Trim the excess fabric from the corner, leaving a ¼" seam allowance. Open the strips and press the seam allowance to one side. Join all strips in this manner.

2 Fold the long binding strip in half lengthwise, right sides together, and press to crease the fold.

3 Trim the batting and backing even with the raw edges of the quilt top. Using a walking foot and a ¼" seam allowance, begin stitching the binding to the right side of the quilt, leaving a 6" tail. Stop stitching ¼" from the corner of the quilt (diagram 28).

diagram 28

4 Lift the needle out of the quilt. Turn the quilt to stitch the next side. Fold the binding up and away from the quilt, with raw edges aligned. Fold the binding back down onto itself, even with the edge of the quilt top. Stitch as before. Repeat the process on the remaining edges and corners of the quilt (diagram 29).

5 On the last side of the quilt, stop stitching about 7" from where you began. Overlap the ending binding tail with the starting tail. Trim the binding ends with a perpendicular cut so that the overlap is exactly the same distance as

diagram 29

the cut width of the binding strips. (If your binding is cut 2½" wide, the overlap should be 2½".)

6 Open up the folded ends of the binding and stitch them, right sides together, as you did to join the original binding strips. Trim the excess corner fabric, refold the binding, and stitch in place. Fold the binding to the back of the quilt and hand stitch in place to cover the binding seam allowance.

Using four separate pieces

1 Measure the quilt through the center from top to bottom. Cut two binding pieces to this length. (If the quilt is large, you may need to join strips to get the appropriate length.)

2 Fold the strips in half lengthwise, wrong sides together, press; then pin and stitch them to the sides of the quilt, easing to fit. Fold the binding to the back and hand stitch in place.

diagram 30

3 Measure the center of the quilt from side to side and add ½" to this measurement. Cut two binding pieces to this length. Turn under ¼" at each short end, then pin and stitch the strips to the top and bottom of the quilt as before (diagram 30).

Hanging sleeve

If your quilt or wall hanging is going to be hung, whether at an exhibition or at home, you will need a hanging sleeve. With a little thought, a sleeve can be added at the binding stage with fabric saved from the backing of the quilt.

1 Cut the fabric 10" x the width of your quilt. Trim under a small hem at each short end and stitch in place.

diagram 31

2 Fold the sleeve in half lengthwise, wrong sides together, and align the raw edges with the top back edge of the quilt before binding. When the binding is stitched in place, it will attach the raw edge of the sleeve (diagram 31).

3 Hand stitch the folded edge into position on the back.

If you want a temporary sleeve, I recommend a piece of fabric that is hand stitched on after completing the binding.

Labeling

Always add a fabric label to your quilt to record details, such as your name, the date, and the title of the piece.

Daisy Chain

DESIGNED BY

Alison Wood

Daisies scattered on the green grass give a summer freshness to this bed topper or throw, which would look good when used in the garden or conservatory. The finished blocks are large at 12" square, and the appliqué shapes are simple, so the quilt goes together quickly for maximum impact with relatively little effort.

MATERIALS

All fabrics used in the quilt are 42" wide, 100% cotton

Daisy petals, centers, and chain blocks:
2 yards of white
1 yard of yellow

Background, borders, and binding:
4½ yards of green

Backing: 4½ yards

Batting: 78" x 92"

Fusible web: 3 yards

CUTTING

1 From the yellow fabric, cut:
2 strips, 2½" x 42"
4 strips, 4½" x 42"; crosscut these strips into
   27 squares, 4½" x 4½"

2 From the white fabric, cut:
2 strips, 2½" x 42"
4 strips, 4½" x 42"; crosscut these strips into
   27 squares, 4½" x 4½"

3 From the green fabric, cut:
7 strips, 4½" x 42"; crosscut these strips into
   54 squares, 4½" x 4½"
4 strips, 12½" x 42"; crosscut these strips into
   12 background squares, 12½" x 12½"

4 From the *remaining* green fabric, cut:
4 border strips, 6½" x the length of fabric
5 binding strips, 2½" x the length of fabric

Quilt plan

Finished size: 72" x 72"

MAKING THE DAISY BLOCKS

1 For the 12 daisy appliqué blocks, enlarge the daisy petals pattern on page 20, then trace 12 daisy petals and 12 daisy centers onto the paper-backed side of the fusible web. Cut out, leaving a ¼" allowance outside the marked lines. Press the fusible-web daisy centers onto the wrong side of the remaining yellow fabric and the fusible-web petal shapes onto the wrong side of the remaining white fabric. Cut out exactly on the marked lines on the fusible web.

2 Remove the paper from the back of one of the white daisy petals and place the shape, right side up, in the center of the right side of one of the 12½" green squares.

3 Remove the paper from the back of one of the yellow daisy centers and place the shape, right side up, in the center of the white daisy petal shape. Press in place. Repeat with the remaining 11 daisy blocks.

4 Using white thread, stitch a small decorative zigzag around the daisy petal shapes, sewing as close as possible to the edge. (See "Hints and Tips for Appliqué by Machine" on page 11.) Do the same with the yellow centers using yellow thread. Repeat for all the daisy appliqué blocks.

MAKING THE CHAIN BLOCKS

1 For each chain block, one center four-patch unit is needed. Using a ¼" seam allowance, stitch one 2½" white strip and one 2½" yellow strip, right sides together, along the length of the strips. Repeat with the other pair of white and yellow 2½" strips. Press the seams toward the yellow fabric.

NOTE

Careful attention to pressing at this stage will give accurate blocks. Press the seams joining the strips flat first, i.e. with the strips still right sides together. This "sets" the seam, causing the thread to sink into the fabric a little which helps to give a flatter, crisper finish. Then, use the side of the iron and flip the top strip open, pressing from the right side to ensure there are no little pleats beside the seams. Try to press, not to iron back and forth, because you do not want to curve the stitched strips.

---

2 Place one pair of stitched strips on top of another pair, alternating the yellow and white fabrics. Align the seam allowances along the length of the strips; they should butt together. Crosscut the strips into 13 segments, each 2½" wide (diagram 1).

diagram 1

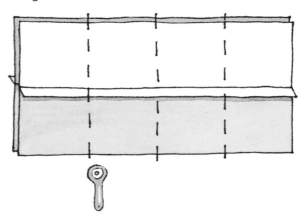

APPLIQUÉ PATTERNS

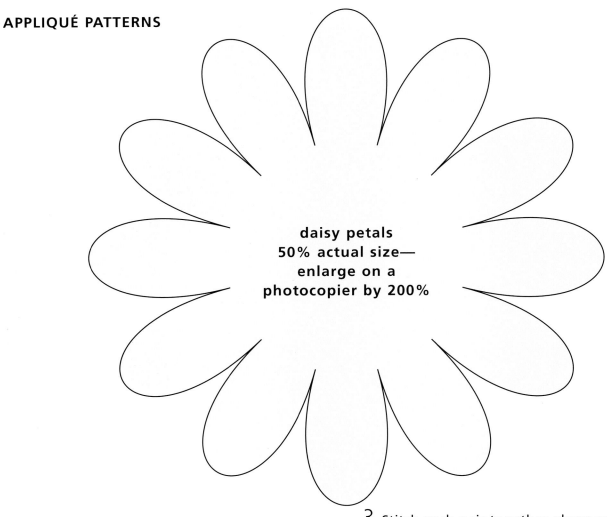

daisy petals
50% actual size—
enlarge on a
photocopier by 200%

daisy center
full size

3 Stitch each pair together along one long side with the top seam facing toward the needle; this will help the seam allowances to butt together and gives a well-matched intersection in the center of the four-patch unit. Make 13 four-patch units. Press the seams toward the yellow fabric; see the note on page 21 for reducing bulk in the center of the block (diagram 2).

diagram 2

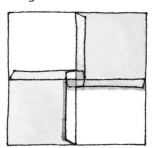

NOTE

To reduce the bulk in the center of a block and to make quilting much easier, try this trick with seam allowances. It is very easy to do provided your stitch length is not too short. Hold a four-patch unit, wrong side up, and with the horizontal seam pointing at an angle away from you, gently pull the section of seam allowance on the right-hand side of the patch toward you with your right thumb and index finger, while keeping the left-hand seam allowance pushed away from you. A few stitches in the seam allowance should pop open, allowing the seams to lie in opposite directions (diagram 2, page 20). Press. I am grateful to Harriet Hargrave, inspirational quiltmaker and teacher, for showing me this trick with the seam allowance.

4 Pin and stitch the 4½" yellow, green, and white squares together using a ¼" seam allowance to make 26 units of three squares each. Press the seam allowances toward the middle green squares.

5 Pin and stitch 4½" green squares on both sides of each four-patch unit (diagram 3). Make a total of 13 of these units. Press th seam allowances toward the green squares.

6 Pin and stitch units made in step 4 on both sides of a unit made in step 5, reversing the direction at top and bottom so that the yellow and the white squares form diagonal patterns to make the chain block. Make a total of 13 chain blocks in this way. Press the seam allowances toward the outside of the blocks (diagram 3).

diagram 3

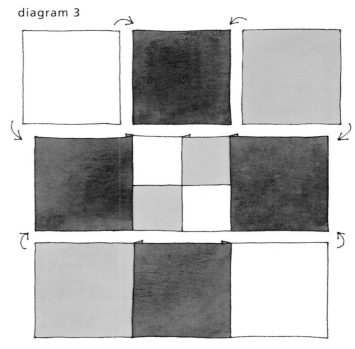

7 Following the quilt plan on page 18, assemble the blocks in five rows of five blocks each, alternating the chain blocks with the daisy appliqué blocks and ensuring that the yellow and white chains connect across the diagonals. Pin and stitch the blocks into rows using a ¼" seam allowance. Press the seams toward the daisy blocks.

8 Stitch the five rows together, carefully matching seams. When stitching, make sure that the underneath seam allowances are lying flat. When all rows have been joined, press all seams in one direction.

ADDING THE BORDERS

1 Measure the pieced top through the center from top to bottom. Trim two of the border strips to this measurement. Pin and stitch these borders to the sides of the pieced top. Press the seams toward the borders.

2 Measure the pieced top through the center from side to side; then trim the remaining two border strips to this measurement. Pin and stitch these borders to the top and bottom of the quilt top. Press as before.

FINISHING

1 Spread the backing right side down on a flat surface, then smooth out the batting and the patchwork top, right side up, on top. Baste together in a grid with safety pins or thread.

2 Machine quilt first along the diagonals of the yellow and white chains to crisscross the quilt. Use thread to match the color of the chain. Stitch parallel lines through the green portions of the chain block using green thread. Extend the quilting into the borders and across the corners of the daisy blocks. Finally, quilt with yellow thread around the daisy centers to secure the middle of each block.

3 Trim any excess batting and backing so they are even with the pieced top. Join the binding strips with diagonal seams to make a continuous length to fit all around the quilt; bind the edges with a double-fold binding, mitered at the corners (see page 14).

Alternative color schemes

1 Pink petals on a soft lavender background make a pretty pastel quilt. **2** Liberty florals sparkle against white; make each daisy different to showcase a collection of small prints. **3** Funky prints on a dark background create a lively version of the design. **4** Yellow daisies with dark centers show that country colors can work just as well as brights or pastels.

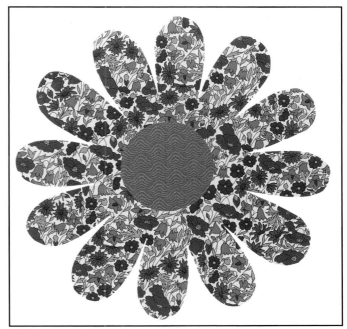

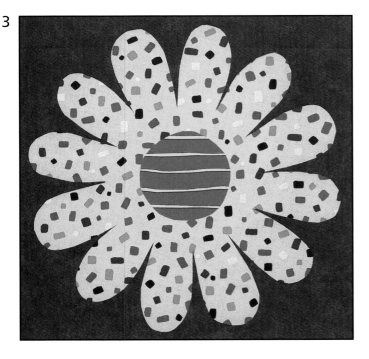

Bright Stars

DESIGNED BY

Sarah Wellfair

This simple but effective design gains its impact from the mixing up of stars and squares in four colors; no two squares have the same color combination. It makes a lively throw to brighten up your sofa or could be used as a topper on a child's bed.

MATERIALS

All fabrics used in the quilt are 42" wide, 100% cotton

Blocks and stars: ⅝ yard each of purple, green, pink, and yellow

Borders: ⅞ yard of light purple

Binding: ½ yard of green

Backing: 1⅝ yards of bright pink

Batting: 44" x 54"

Fusible web: 1⅛ yards

CUTTING

1 From *each* of the block and star fabrics, cut:
1 strip, 10½" x 42"; crosscut each strip into
3 squares, 10½" x 10½" (12 squares total)

2 From the remaining star fabrics, cut 3 stars from each, as follows. Use the pattern on page 28 to trace 12 stars onto the smooth side of fusible web, leaving a ¼" allowance all around each star. Cut out the shapes just outside the marked lines. Press 3 star shapes onto the wrong side of each of the remaining purple, green, pink, and yellow fabrics. Cut out the stars accurately along the marked lines.

3 From the light purple fabric, cut:
5 border strips, 5" x 42"

4 From the green fabric, cut:
5 binding strips, 3" x 42"

25

Quilt plan

Finished size: 40" x 50"

STITCHING

1 Following the quilt plan on page 26, position one star in the center of each of the purple, green, pink, and yellow squares. Each star should go on each of three different-colored fabrics so that no two color combinations are the same. Remove the paper from the back of the stars and press to fuse them in place.

2 Stitch a large close zigzag in black thread all around the edge of each star. When turning a corner, drop the needle over the edge into the background fabric, lift the presser foot, and pivot the fabric on the needle until it's in the correct position to stitch the next edge.

3 Arrange the squares in rows of three different colors as desired (see quilt plan) and stitch, right sides together, using a ¼" seam allowance (diagram 1). Then stitch the four rows, right sides together. Press the seams toward the darker fabrics.

diagram 1

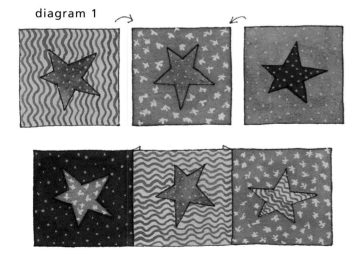

ADDING THE BORDERS

1 Measure the pieced top through the center from side to side; then trim two of the light purple border strips to this length. Pin and stitch them to the top and bottom of the quilt.

2 Measure the pieced top through the center from top to bottom. Sew the three remaining border strips together and then cut two borders from the long strip to this measurement. Pin and stitch them to the sides of the quilt.

FINISHING

1 Trim the backing and batting to 2" larger than the pieced top on all sides. Spread the backing right side down on a flat surface, then smooth out the batting and the pieced top, right side up, on top. Baste together in a grid with safety pins or thread.

2 Machine quilt in a stippling design around the stars using invisible thread. Leave the borders free, or quilt as desired.

3 Trim any excess batting and backing so they are even with the pieced top. Stitch the binding strips end to end to make a continuous length to fit around the quilt; bind the edges with a double-fold binding, mitered at the corners (see page 14).

**APPLIQUÉ PATTERN
full size**

star

Alternative color schemes

1 A dark check with pale blue stars makes a good masculine colorway. 2 Teddy bears and gold stars are perfect for toddlers. 3 A red-and-beige color scheme gives a homespun look. 4 Black and white fabrics produce a striking, graphic colorway.

Leaf Wall Hanging

DESIGNED BY

Gail Smith

This wall hanging is inspired by the leafy countryside near my home and the vibrant colors of autumn. It will brighten your home even on the dullest winter day. The embellished panels add a textured finish, and the quilt features different types of leaves: machine appliquéd, machine embroidered, raw-edge appliquéd, and machine quilted.

MATERIALS

All fabrics used in the quilt are 42" wide, 100% cotton

Block background: 1¼ yards of cream print

Block background: ½ yard of mustard yellow

Embellished panels: ½ yard of multicolored pink/orange/yellow

Sashing and panels:
⅜ yard of marbled orange
⅛ yard of cranberry

Batik panels and binding: ⅝ yard of pink/orange

Appliqué leaves:
⅓ yard of lime green
⅓ yard of light green
¼ yard of tan
⅛ yard of bronze metallic

Backing and hanging sleeve: 3 yards

Batting: 45" x 53"

Fusible web: 1½ yards

CUTTING

Label all pieces for reference.

1 From the cream fabric, cut:
10½" x 11½" (block 1)
13¼" x 26¼" (block 2)
9½" x 16½" (block 5)
12½" x 11½" (block 6)
12½" x 19½" (block 7)
Plan the cutting carefully to fit the fabric (see quilt plan on page 32).

2 From the mustard yellow fabric, cut:
13½" x 12½" (block 3)
10½" x 10½" (block 4)

3 From the multicolored fabric, cut:
3¼" x 11½" (piece 1a—attaches to block 1)
13¼" x 6" (piece 2a—attaches to block 2)
12½" x 11" (piece 6a—attaches to block 6)

4 From the marbled orange fabric, cut:
13¼" x 4" (piece 1b—attaches to block 1)
12½" x 6¼" (piece 7a—attaches to block 7)
4 strips, 2" x 13½", for block 4 sashing

Quilt plan

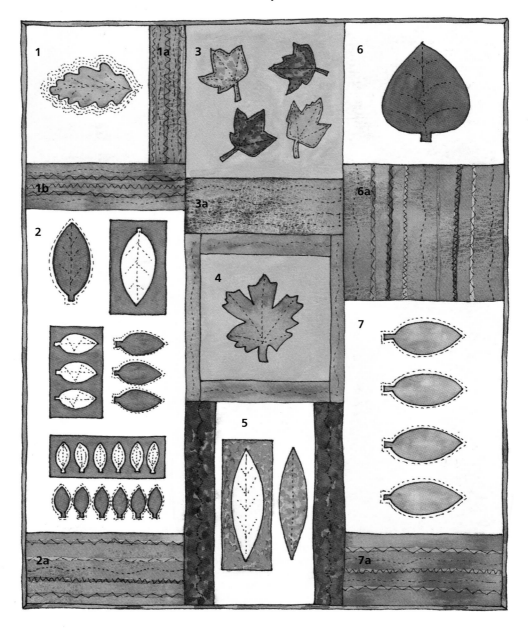

Finished size: 38" x 47"

5 From the cranberry fabric, cut:
  2 pieces, 2½" x 16½", for block 5 sashing

6 From the batik fabric, cut:
  13½" x 5¼" (piece 3a)
  5 binding strips, 2½" x 42"

ASSEMBLING THE QUILT TOP

1 Use the patterns on pages 34 through 36 to trace the appliqué leaf shapes onto the smooth side of fusible web. You can use the leaf shapes as is, or reverse some of them if desired (see quilt plan). Cut out just outside the marked lines and then press the fusible web shapes to the wrong side of the appropriate pieces of fabric. Cut out the shapes exactly on the marked lines on the fusible web.

NOTE

Some of the leaf patterns are enclosed in a box; these are used as both positive and negative images cut from the same piece of fabric. Cut them out as accurately as possible. To start cutting, fold the fabric in half and make a small cut at the fold using pointed scissors (diagram 1). Open out and continue cutting around the shape.

diagram 1

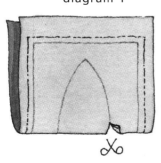

2 Remove the paper from the back of the leaf shapes and position the leaves right side up on each background block as shown in the quilt plan, opposite. Press the shapes in place.

3 Using matching threads, stitch around each leaf shape as follows, but do not add the leaf veins at this stage:

blocks 1 and 7: blanket stitch;
blocks 2, 4, and 5: satin stitch;
blocks 3 and 6: edge stitch close to the edge using a straight stitch.

4 Embellish the multicolored panels (pieces 1a, 2a, 6a) with machine embroidery using thick wool or thread; couch the thread in rows onto the fabric (diagram 2). Repeat with the two marbled orange panels (pieces 1b and 7a). Leave piece 3a between blocks 3 and 4 blank for now. (See "Couching" on page 11.)

diagram 2

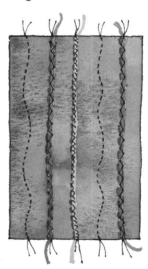

5 Pin and stitch a marbled orange sashing strip, right sides together, to one side of block 4. Use a ¼" seam allowance and repeat on all four sides of the block, trimming as necessary. Pin and stitch the cranberry sashing strips to the long sides of block 5 in the same manner. Press all seams toward the darker fabrics.

6 Pin and stitch block 1, the oak leaf, to its side panel (piece 1a) using a ¼" seam allowance. Attach piece 1b to the bottom of block 1 in the same manner. Continue joining the blocks and sashing pieces together in this manner, making three columns. Be sure to follow the numerical order of the blocks (see quilt plan).

7 Pin and stitch the three columns together, easing to fit. Press all seams toward the darker fabrics.

FINISHING

1 Piece the backing and then spread it right side down on a flat surface. Smooth out the batting and the pieced top, right side up, on top. Baste together in a grid with safety pins or thread.

2 Use a walking foot and straight stitch to add quilted veins to the leaves (see dotted lines on patterns). Add extra stitching in between the rows of embellishments on pieces 1a, 2a, and 6a, and wavy lines in the panel (piece 3a) between blocks 3 and 4. Quilt in the ditch around each block if desired. Quilt around the leaf shapes on blocks 1, 2, 5, 6, and 7.

3 Stitch the binding strips with diagonal seams to make a continuous length to fit all around the quilt. Bind the edges with a double-fold binding, mitered at the corners.

4 Use the leftover backing fabric to add a hanging sleeve at this stage (see page 15).

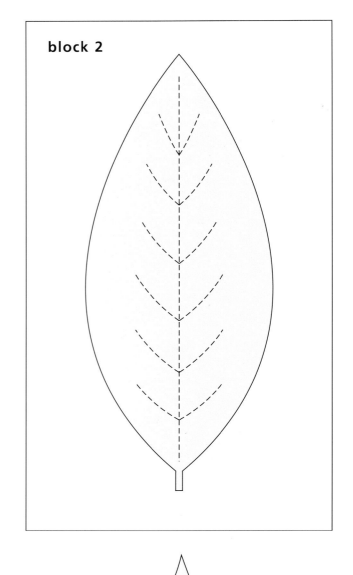

block 2

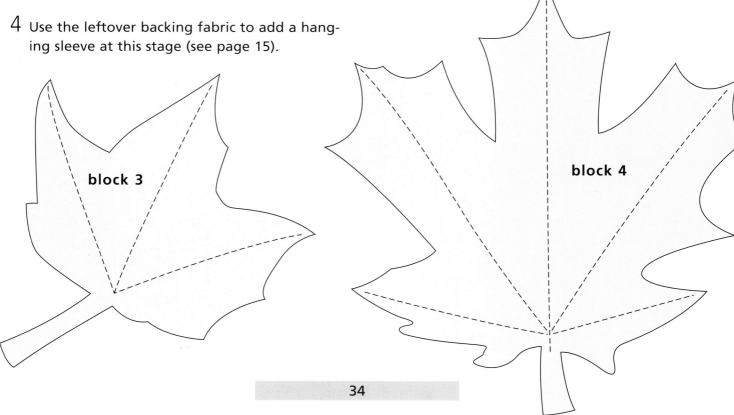

block 3

block 4

APPLIQUÉ PATTERNS
All patterns are 75% of actual size. Enlarge on a photocopier 133%.

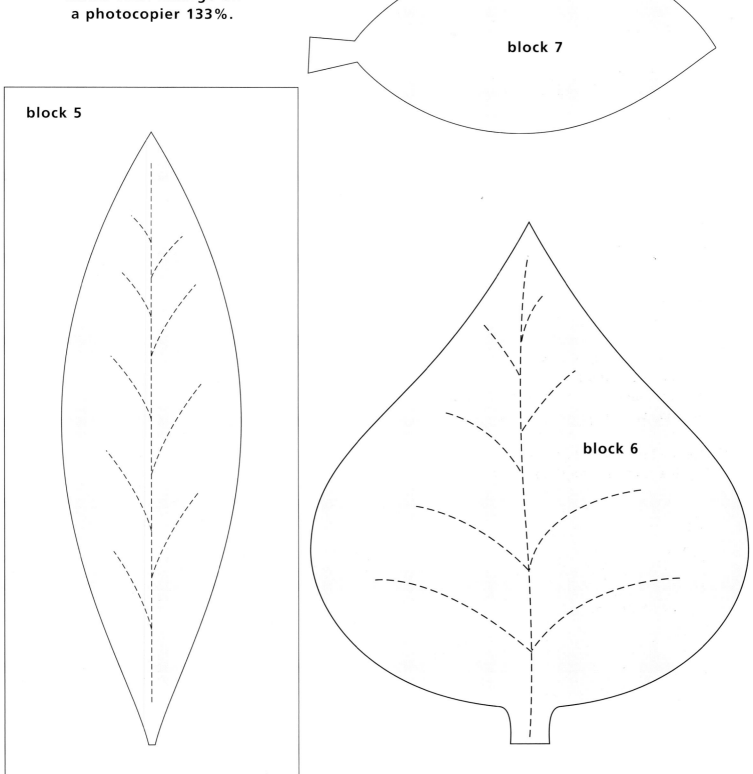

block 5

block 6

block 7

APPLIQUÉ PATTERNS
All patterns are 75% of
actual size. Enlarge on
a photocopier 133%.

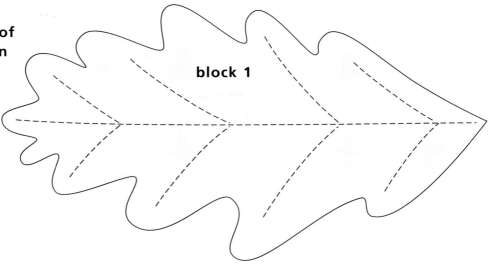

block 1

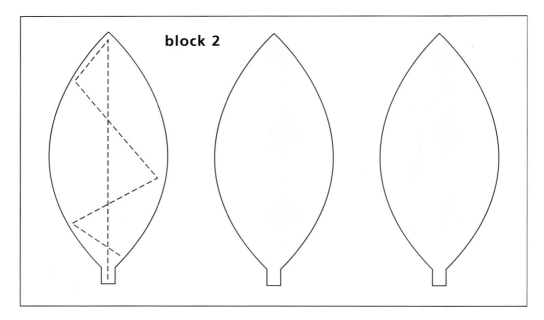

block 2

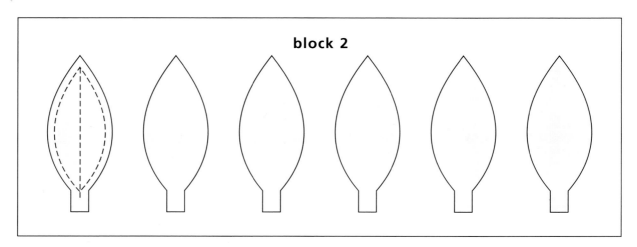

block 2

Alternative color schemes

1 Soft flannels in warm colors give a soft, cozy feel to the quilt, perfect for winter.
2 This warm color scheme features a lively green for a bit of zing. 3 Choose fabrics printed with a hint of metallic gold to give a rich, regal feel to the quilt. 4 This purple color scheme has a more feminine feel and hints at heather in the countryside.

1

2

3

4

A Touch of Spice

DESIGNED BY

Nikki Foley

The design for this quilt was inspired by nineteenth-century artwork in an Indian palace. The white background with bold appliquéd shapes is complimented by gold machine quilting, and the hand-quilted spirals capture the very essence of Indian style.

MATERIALS

All fabrics used in the quilt are 42" wide, 100% cotton

Blocks and outer border:
2 yards of white tone-on-tone print

Appliqué:
⅓ yard each of bright pink and royal blue

Sashing and binding:
1⅓ yards of turquoise

Backing: 3 yards

Batting: 54" x 67"

Fusible web: ½ yard

Gold and turquoise threads for machine quilting

Gold pearl cotton for hand quilting

CUTTING

1 From the white fabric, cut:
4 strips, 12" x 42"; crosscut into 12 squares, 12" x 12"
5 border strips, 3" x 42"

2 From the turquoise fabric, cut:
11 strips, 2½" x 42"; crosscut 6 of the strips into 12" lengths to make 16 short sashing strips
6 binding strips, 2½" x 42"

3 For the appliqué shapes, use pattern A on page 41 to trace 24 shapes onto the smooth side of the fusible web. Likewise, trace 12 shapes using pattern B, and 24 shapes using pattern C. Carefully cut out each shape just outside the marked lines and place them as follows onto the wrong side of the fabrics: A shapes on the pink fabric, B and C shapes on the royal blue fabric. Press the shapes into place. Cut out the shapes accurately along the marked lines.

Quilt plan

Finished size: 47½" x 61"

STITCHING

1 Position the appliqué shapes onto the 12"
white squares. You will need six of each
design (diagram 1). Align the straight edges
of the royal blue semicircles with the edges of
the white squares so that they will be incor-
porated in the seam allowances. Peel off the
paper backing from the prepared shapes and
press in place. Using matching thread, stitch a
zigzag or other decorative stitch around the
edges of the appliqué shapes.

diagram 1

 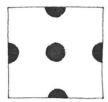

NOTE

To find the center of each square for positioning the
appliqué shapes accurately, fold each square in half
horizontally and finger-press, then open and fold in
half vertically and again finger-press. The center will be
where the two creases meet.

2 Pin and stitch the shorter turquoise sashing
strips to each side of the white appliquéd
squares (diagram 2), right sides together,
using a ¼" seam allowance. Following the
quilt plan on page 40, make four rows, alternating the pink appliqué with the royal blue.
Press all seams toward the sashing.

diagram 2

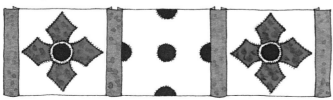

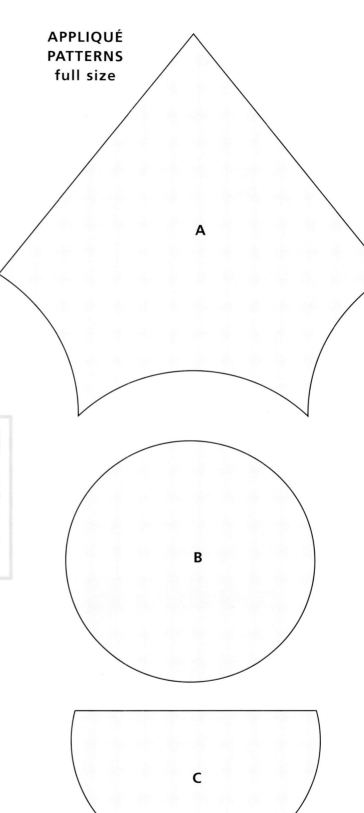

A

B

C

3 Pin and stitch long turquoise sashing strips to the top and bottom of the first row using a ¼" seam allowance. Trim the ends and press the seam allowances toward the turquoise. Pin and stitch the next row to the bottom edge of the turquoise strip. Pin and stitch another long sashing strip to the bottom of this row. Repeat to join the remaining rows with sashing strips, ending with a sashing strip. Trim and press as you go.

ADDING THE BORDERS

1 Measure the pieced top through the center from side to side; then trim two of the 3" white border strips to this measurement. Pin and stitch to the top and bottom of the quilt.

2 Stitch the remaining 3" white border strips together. Measure the pieced top through the center from top to bottom; then cut two strips to this measurement. Pin and stitch to the quilt sides.

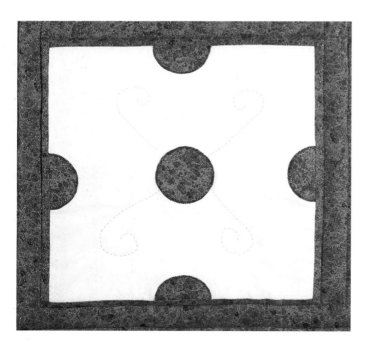

FINISHING

1 Lay the quilt top on a flat surface right side up; then, using a quilter's pencil, mark the spiral quilting design freehand on the squares with the blue circles.

2 Piece the backing and then spread it right side down on a flat surface. Smooth the batting and quilt top, right side up, on top. Baste together in a grid with safety pins or thread.

3 Use a walking foot and gold thread to machine quilt the inside edge of each pink appliquéd square; stitch two lines of decorative stitches on either side of the border. Using a matching thread, straight stitch along the turquoise sashing. Hand quilt the spirals on each blue appliquéd square using gold pearl cotton (diagram 3).

diagram 3

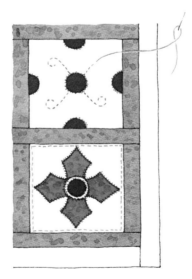

4 Trim any excess batting and backing so they are even with the pieced top. Join the binding strips with diagonal seams to make a continuous length to fit all around the quilt; bind the edges with a double-fold binding, mitered at the corners.

Alternative color schemes

1 Red, yellow and green on white background are stunning. 2 Black-and-white is an ideal color plan for a boy's room. 3 Pink and purple on a dark background create a dramatic atmosphere. 4 Pastel colors guarantee a soft impression.

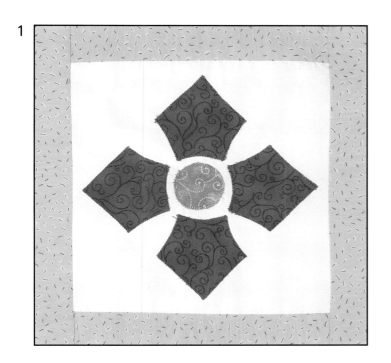

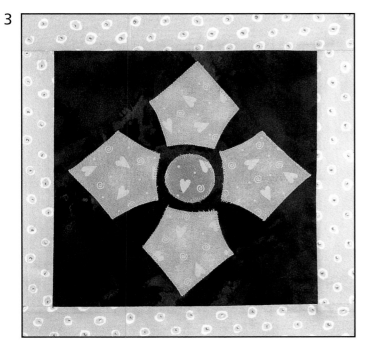

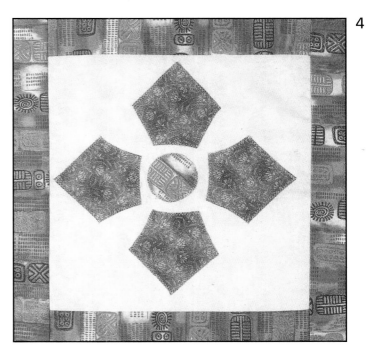

Noshi Wall Hanging

DESIGNED BY

Dorothy Wood

This appliqué design is named *Noshi* after the Japanese talisman that is tradition-
ally made from strips of abalone, a marine mollusk. The strips are tied together with
pretty lengths of paper and attached to gifts at New Year as an emblem of good
fortune. The quilt pattern was inspired by square-paneled screens that are
known in Japan as shoji, and has been designed as a wall hanging.

MATERIALS

All fabrics used in the quilt are 42" wide,
100% cotton

Appliqué: Japanese prints as follows:
4 fat quarters (18" x 22") of dark blue
3 fat quarters of cream
1 fat quarter of red

Background, sashing, and binding:
1¼ yards of cream

Backing: ⅞ yard

Batting: 27" x 27"

Fusible web: 1 yard

CUTTING

From the cream fabric, cut:
   9 squares, 7¼" x 7¼"
   6 rectangles, 2" x 7¼"
   2 rectangles, 2" x 23¾"
   4 border strips, 3½" x 42"
   1 hanging-tab strip, 3⅜" x 40"

ASSEMBLING THE QUILT TOP

1 Enlarge the block patterns on page 48 as
   directed. Trace the full-sized appliqué shapes
   onto fusible web. Mark the block numbers
   and colors onto each shape (diagram 1). Cut
   out the shapes just outside the lines.

diagram 1

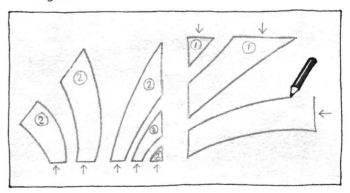

Quilt plan

Finished size: 26¼" x 26¼"

2 Press each fusible-web shape to the wrong side of the appropriate Japanese fabric. Cut out the appliqué shapes from the fabric along the marked lines. Following the quilt plan, opposite, arrange the appliqués so that the designs will flow from one square to another on the finished quilt.

3 Lay a 7¼" square of cream fabric over each block pattern. Remove the papers from the back of the appliqué shapes and position them on the cream squares following the guidelines of the pattern below (see quilt plan, opposite). Press each shape with an iron to secure.

APPLIQUÉ PATTERNS

Patterns are quarter size.
Enlarge on a photocopier by 200%, then by 200% again,
so that each block is 7¼" square.

4 Machine stitch a narrow satin stitch along the edges of each dark blue appliqué piece using dark blue embroidery thread. Change to cream embroidery thread and satin stitch the edges of the cream print pieces. Change to deep red thread to satin stitch the remaining red pieces (see diagram 2).

diagram 2

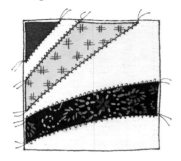

5 Press the panels and trim any thread ends.

6 Pin and stitch the appliquéd blocks to the shorter sashing strips to form three rows of three blocks; use a ¼" seam allowance. Press the seams toward the sashing strips (diagram 3). Then join the three rows of blocks using the two longer sashing strips. Take care to align the squares from one row to the next as you pin the rows together. Press all the seams toward the sashing.

diagram 3

ADDING THE BORDERS

1 Measure the pieced top through the center from top to bottom; then trim two of the 3½" cream border strips to this measurement. Stitch them to the sides of the quilt top.

2 Measure the pieced top through the center from side to side; then trim the remaining 3½" cream border strips to this measurement. Stitch these strips to the top and bottom of the quilt.

3 Press under ¼" along the outer edges of each border strip. Then fold the strips in half lengthwise, wrong sides together, and press. Open out.

FINISHING

1 Spread the pieced top right side down on a flat surface. Trim the batting to 27" x 27" and smooth it out on top, aligning it with the pressed lines on the border strips. Trim the backing to 23¾" x 23¾" and position it right side up on top of the batting (diagram 4). Baste together in a grid with safety pins or thread.

diagram 4

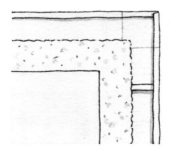

diagram 5

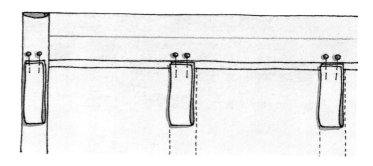

2 Quilt in the ditch around each quilt block.

3 Fold the 3⅜"-wide cream tab strip in half lengthwise, right sides together. Stitch the raw edges together along the length of the strip using a ¼" seam allowance. Turn the tube right side out and press, centering the seam in the middle. Crosscut into four pieces, each 10" long.

4 Fold the cream *side* border strips to the backside of the quilt and slip-stitch in place to create binding. Lay the folded tabs with the loop facing down evenly across the top, matching the quilting lines and side borders (diagram 5). Pin so the top of the tab is level with the raw edges of the binding turning. Hand stitch across the end of the tabs to secure.

5 Fold over the top and bottom border strips to the reverse side and slip-stitch in place. Fold the tabs up and slip stitch them securely along the top edge of the quilt.

Alternative color schemes

1 Use bold primary and secondary colors to create a bright, contemporary design. 2 Coordinating polka-dot fabrics and plain fabrics make a fun quilt.
3 Select one or two multicolored prints and pick out colors from it to complete the design. 4 Choose a variety of prints in the same colorway for a soothing design.

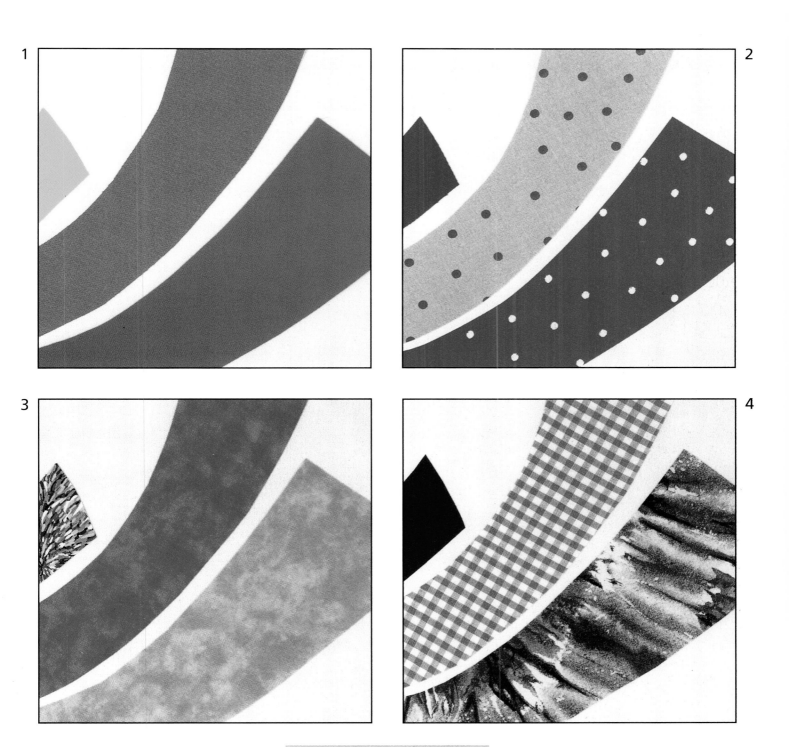

Butterflies

DESIGNED BY

Sarah Wellfair

I based this design on the pretty little Adonis Blue butterfly, and worked the appliqué in a variety of colors and in two sizes to give a sense of movement to the design. This quilt makes a cheery throw for a sunroom.

MATERIALS

All fabrics used in the quilt are 42" wide, 100% cotton

Background fabric: 1 yard of cream

Butterfly wings: ⅝ yard each of pink, lilac, and yellow,

Butterfly bodies: fat quarter (18" x 22") of dark blue

Sashing: ⅝ yard of lilac

Borders: ⅝ yard of yellow

Binding: ½ yard of pink

Backing: 3 yards

Batting: 45" x 49"

Fusible web: 1⅛ yards

CUTTING

1 From the cream fabric, cut:
3 strips, 10½" x 30½"

2 From the lilac fabric, cut:
4 sashing strips, 2½" x 30½"
2 sashing strips, 2½" x 38½"

3 From the yellow fabric, cut:
2 border strips, 3½" x 34½"
3 border strips, 3½" x 42"

4 From the pink fabric, cut:
5 binding strips, 3" x 42"

ASSEMBLING THE QUILT TOP

1 Use the applique patterns A, B, C, and D on page 56 to trace nine pairs of large wings and three pairs of small wings onto the smooth side of fusible web, allowing ¼" around each shape. Use patterns E and F to trace nine large and three small butterfly bodies. Cut out the shapes just outside the marked lines. Press the shapes onto the wrong side of each of the fabric colors following the quilt plan on page 54, and then cut out exactly along the marked lines.

Quilt plan

Finished size: 44" x 40"

2 Working on one background panel at a time, position the butterfly shapes following the quilt plan above. You will need three large butterflies and one small one for each panel.

3 Remove the papers from the back of the butterfly wing fabrics and press in place, right side up, on each background panel. Remove

the papers from the back of the butterfly bodies and press the bodies over the wings to fuse everything in place.

4 Satin stitch along the edges of the butterfly pieces using a narrow zigzag and matching thread. Machine stitch the antennae using dark blue thread. Press all three panels.

5 Pin and stitch a 30½" lilac sashing strip to each side of two of the butterfly panels using a ¼" seam allowance. Pin and stitch the final butterfly panel in between these two panels. Press the seams toward the sashing.

6 Pin and stitch the 38½" sashing strips to the top and bottom of the quilt top (diagram 1). Press the seams toward the lilac fabric.

diagram 1

ADDING THE BORDERS

1 Pin and stitch the 34½" yellow border strips to either side of the quilt top. Press the seams toward the lilac fabric.

2 Join the remaining three border strips end to end, and then measure the pieced top through the center from side to side. Cut two border strips to this measurement. Pin and stitch them to the top and bottom of the quilt top (diagram 2). Press the seams toward the lilac fabric.

diagram 2

FINISHING

1 Spread the backing right side down on a flat surface; then smooth out the batting and the pieced top, right side up, on top. Baste together in a grid with safety pins or thread.

2 Machine quilt around the butterflies using cream thread; then quilt in the ditch around each butterfly panel. Free-motion machine quilt on the cream background fabric and quilt the pattern of your choice in the yellow borders.

3 Stitch the binding strips with diagonal seams to make a continuous length to fit all around the quilt; bind the edges with a double-fold binding, mitered at the corners.

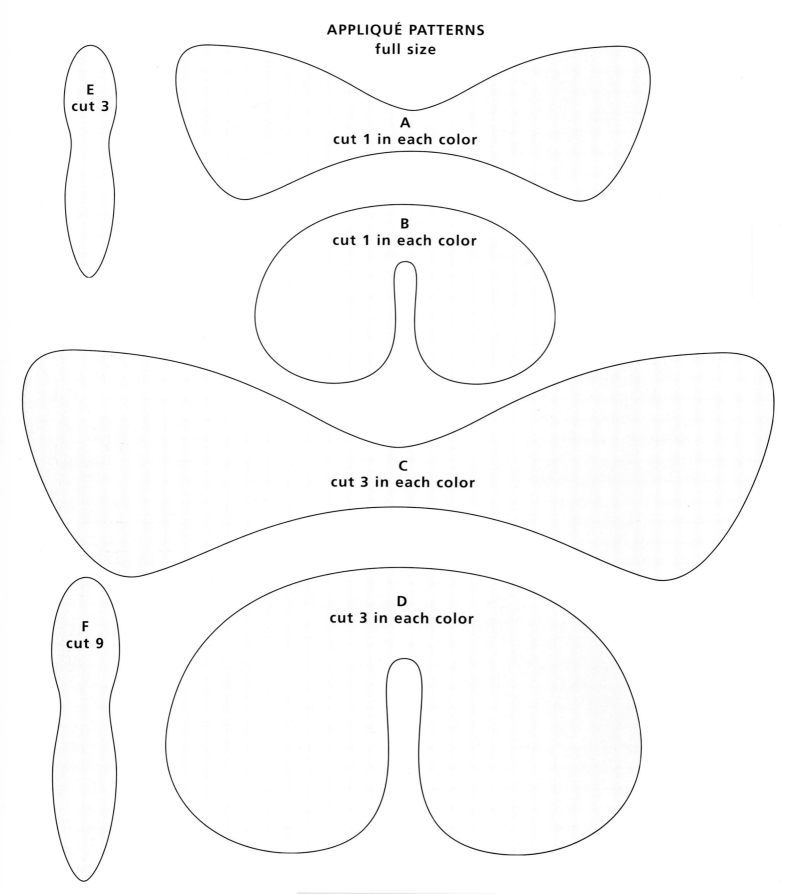

APPLIQUÉ PATTERNS
full size

E
cut 3

A
cut 1 in each color

B
cut 1 in each color

C
cut 3 in each color

D
cut 3 in each color

F
cut 9

Alternative color schemes

1 Blue and white with a touch of silver is a fresh and cool combination. 2 Hand-dyed fabrics in hot colors make a vibrant quilt. 3 The bright green background gives a summery feel to this colorway. 4 Plain fabrics on a mottled background are restful.

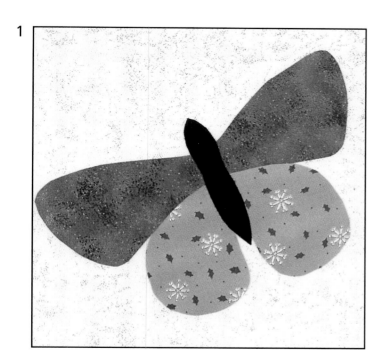

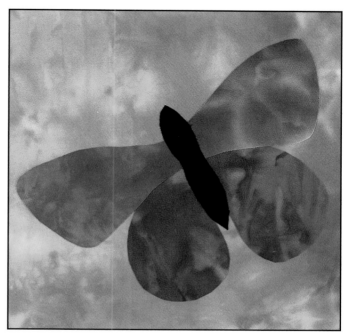

Starflower

DESIGNED BY

Mary O'Riordan

This quilt was inspired by a fabric collection containing an unusual mix of color. New and recycled fabrics have been combined to give an old-fashioned yet exotic feel. The appliqué flowers appear to float on the surface of the quilt and are constructed from a single, simple petal shape.

MATERIALS

All fabrics used in the quilt are 42" wide, 100% cotton

Appliqué:
¼ yard each of mauve and violet

Background fabric and nine-patch blocks:
⅓ yard each of 4 pinks, 4 mauves, 4 pale blues, and 4 lime greens; or scraps to total 1⅓ yards

Borders and binding:
2 yards of cornflower blue print

Backing: 3 yards

Batting: 52" x 63"

Fusible web: 1 yard

Template plastic

CUTTING

1 Trace the petal pattern on page 62 onto template plastic and cut out accurately. Use the template to trace 30 petal shapes onto the smooth side of the fusible web and cut out ¼" around the petal edges (diagram 1). Press 15 of the fusible-web pieces to the wrong side of the mauve appliqué fabric and 15 to the violet applique fabric. Cut out the petals exactly on the marked lines to make six flowers, each with five petals.

diagram 1

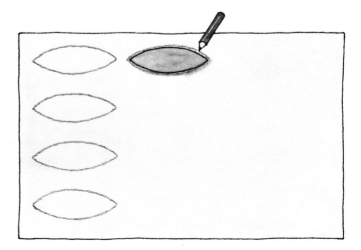

Quilt plan

Finished size: 45½" x 56"

2 From the pinks, mauves, pale blues, and lime
greens, cut:
106 squares (total), 4" x 4"

3 From the cornflower blue print, cut:
4 border strips, 11" x 42"
6 binding strips, 2½" x 42"

STITCHING

1 Using 36 of the 4" squares, make four nine-
patch blocks. Combine the fabrics randomly.
For each block, sew three squares together
for each row. Press the seams in opposite
directions from one row to the next. Then
sew the rows together (diagram 2).

diagram 2

2 Pin and stitch the remaining 70 squares
into 10 rows of 7 squares each. Press the seam
allowances in opposite directions from one
row to the next. Then join the rows to form
the center background for the appliqué
flowers (see quilt plan on page 60).

ADDING THE BORDERS

1 Measure the long sides of the pieced background and trim two of the 11"-wide border
strips to this measurement. Pin and stitch
these to the long sides, easing to fit.

2 Trim the remaining two 11"-wide border
strips to measure 25" and stitch a nine-patch
block to each end. Then pin and stitch these
rows to the top and bottom of the quilt,
matching seams carefully (diagram 3). Press
seams toward the borders.

diagram 3

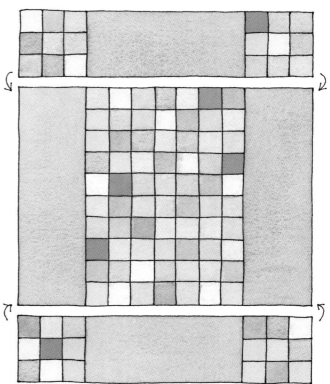

APPLIQUÉ PATTERN
full size

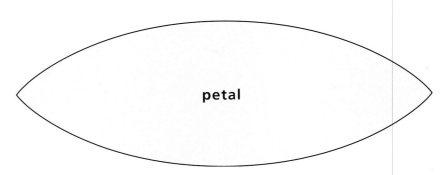

petal

FINISHING

1 Peel off the paper backing from the prepared petals and position them as desired on the quilt top. Press in place. Then using matching thread, stitch a narrow decorative zigzag around the petal shapes, stitching as close as possible to the edge to secure them.

2 Spread the backing right side down on a flat surface. Then smooth out the batting and the pieced top, right side up, on top. Baste the layers together in a grid with safety pins or thread.

3 Beginning at the edge of the pieced block, machine or hand quilt in a grid on the background squares and outline the star flowers. Quilt the border in a continuous vine pattern.

4 Stitch the binding strips with diagonal seams to make a continuous length to fit all around the quilt; bind the edges with a double-fold binding, mitered at the corners.

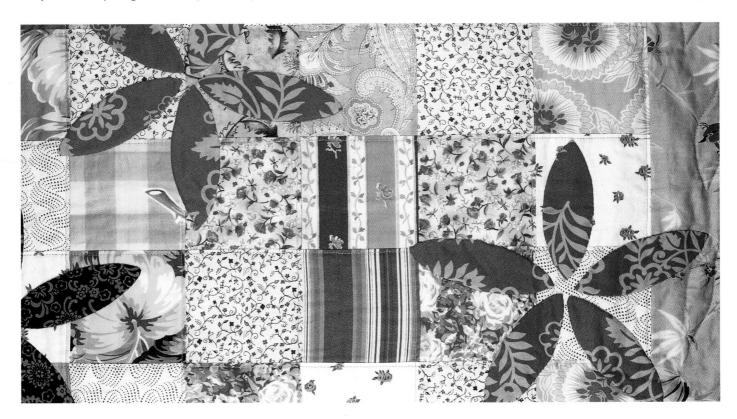

Alternative color schemes

1 Rich autumnal red- and rust-colored fabrics with leaves in golds and browns would make this quilt perfect for hibernation! **2** Use scraps of black-and-white fabric and a different color for each petal for a happy, scrappy quilt. **3** A neutral background will work with almost any favorite fabric for this buttercup-and-blue scheme. **4** Recycled checks and the latest batiks are combined in a low-contrast color scheme.

1

2

3

4

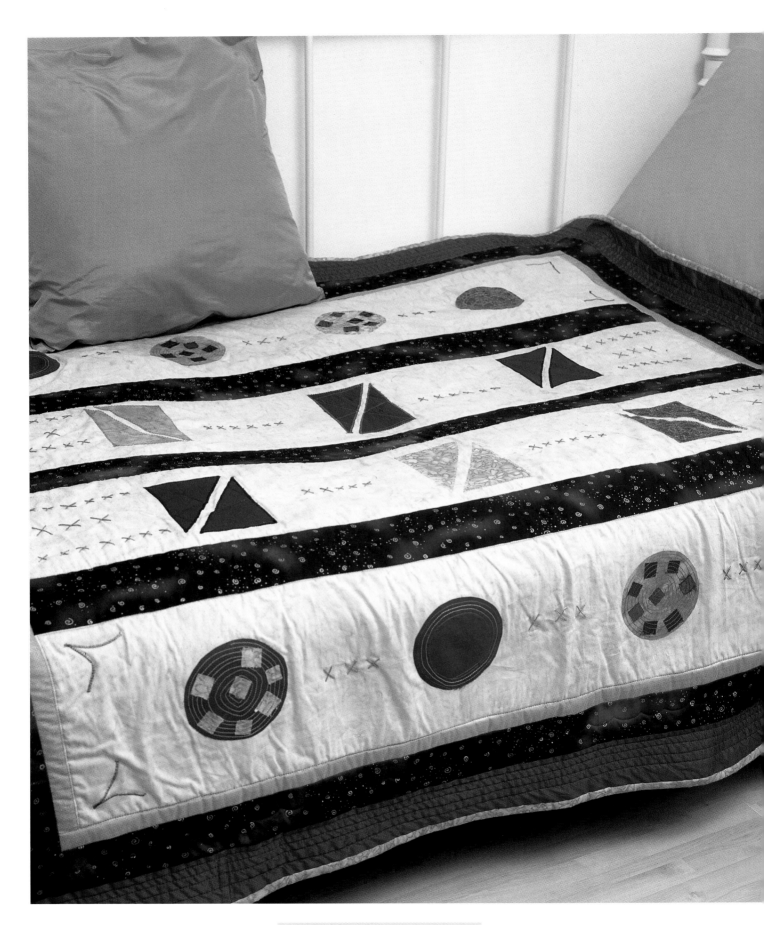

Promenade Throw

DESIGNED BY

Gail Smith

This throw features silk, velvet, and fleece—luxurious fabrics that are not normally used in patchwork. The design comes from an embroidered vest, and is inspired by the parasols, beach huts, and seashells that are found at the seaside. The raw-edge appliqué adds additional texture, while the hand and machine embroidery give further interest. The shape of the throw is perfect for a sofa or futon.

MATERIALS

The cotton, silk, and velvet fabrics are 42" wide; the fleece is 60" wide

Background panels: 1 yard of pink batik

Sashing and middle border: ¾ yard of royal blue cotton with metallic print

Inner border: ¼ yard of turquoise cotton lamé

Outer border: ¼ yard of cherry red silk

Appliqué: fat quarters of 6 different fabrics in cherry red, blue, turquoise, and pink in assorted materials, such as silk, velvet, and cotton

Backing: 1½ yards of pink fleece

Binding: ½ yard of dark pink floral batik

Fusible web: 1 yard

Pink/blue variegated size 5 pearl cotton for embroidery

CUTTING

1 From the pink batik fabric, cut:
4 strips, 8½" x 42"

2 From the royal blue fabric, cut:
3 sashing strips, 3½" x 42"
4 middle-border strips, 2½" x 42"

3 From the turquoise cotton lamé, cut:
4 inner-border strips, 1¼" x 42"

4 From the cherry red silk, cut:
4 outer-border strips, 3½" x 42"

5 From the dark pink floral batik, cut:
5 binding strips, 2½" x 42"

Quilt plan

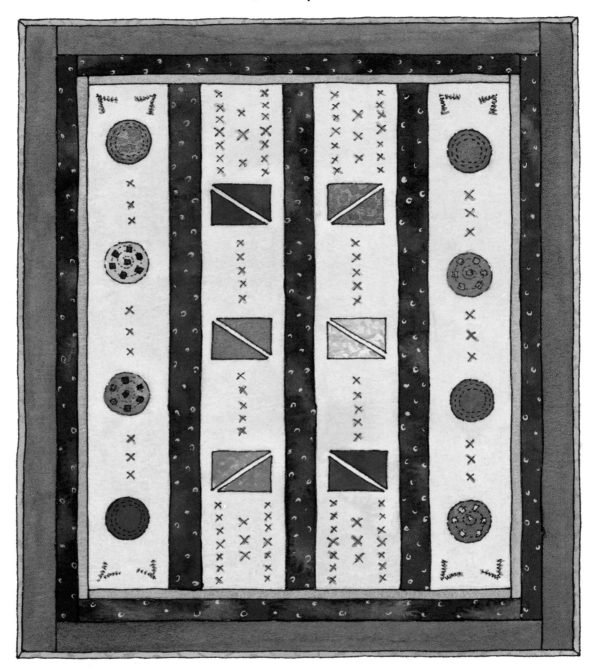

Finished size: 52½" x 53½"

NOTE

If the silk fabric for the border frays, you can prevent this by serging the edges, or using a zigzag or overlock stitch on the edges. The other silk fabric shapes will not fray once the fusible web has been applied to them.

ASSEMBLING THE QUILT TOP

1 Use the patterns on page 69 to trace eight circles and six rectangles onto fusible web. Cut them out just outside the lines (diagram 1).

diagram 1

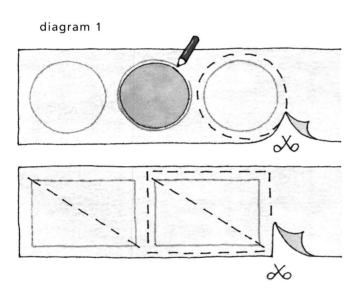

2 Press the fusible-side of the assorted appliqué fabrics. Cut out the shapes exactly on the marked lines. Cut the rectangles in half diagonally as indicated on the pattern to make 12 triangles.

3 To prevent fraying, apply fusible web to the wrong side of the silk and velvet to be used to decorate the appliqué circles. Cut 32 pieces, roughly ¾" square, to decorate four of the appliqué circles.

4 Remove the papers from the back of the appliqué circles and triangles and position them, right side up, on the pink panels, referring to the quilt plan on page 66. Press in place. Remove the papers from the small squares of velvet and silk and press onto the circles in a random pattern (add more small squares if you wish). Use a warm iron so that you won't scorch these fabrics.

5 With matching thread, stitch a spiral pattern onto each circle using your presser foot as a spacing guide. Start at the outer edge and stitch until you reach the center of each circle. On the circles with decorative velvet and silk squares, stitch right over them (diagram 2). You may wish to practice on a sample first.

diagram 2

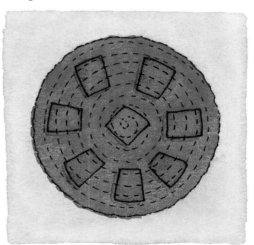

6 Zigzag stitch around the edges of the triangles using matching thread. Bury the thread tails on the back of the panels.

7 Trim the four panels to 42" long. Pin the panels to the three royal blue sashing strips, taking care to align the appliqué patterns across the quilt top.

8 Stitch the panels and sashing strips together using a ¼" seam allownce. Press the seams toward the darker fabric. Trim the sashing strips even with the panels.

APPLIQUÉ PATTERNS
full size

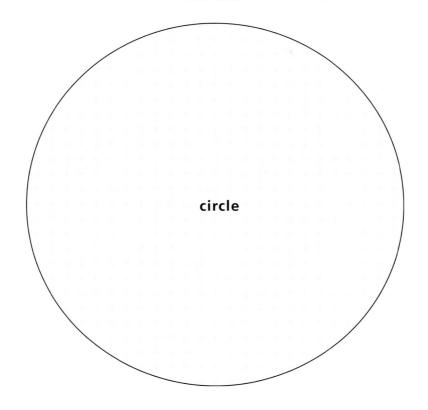

circle

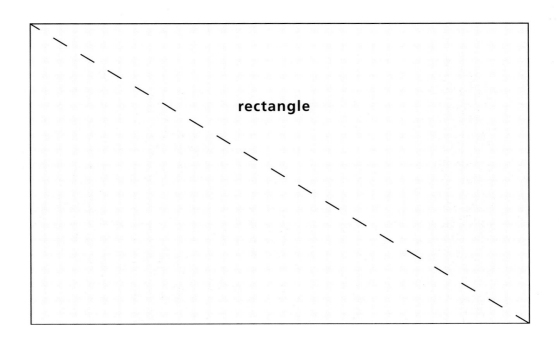

rectangle

ADDING THE BORDERS

1 Press all the seams toward the darker fabrics as you go. Note that silk and cotton lamé need to be pressed at a lower temperature than cotton. Measure the pieced top through the center from side to side; then trim two of the turquoise border strips to this measurement. Pin and stitch them to the top and bottom of the quilt.

2 Measure the pieced top through the center from top to bottom; then trim the remaining two turquoise border strips to this measurement. Pin and stitch them to the quilt sides.

3 Add the middle border in the same way. Measure the pieced top through the center from side to side; then trim two royal blue strips to this measurement. Pin and stitch them to the top and bottom of the quilt. Measure the quilt top through the center from top to bottom; then trim the two remaining royal blue strips to this measurement. Pin and stitch them to the quilt sides.

4 Next, attach the outer border. Pin and stitch three of the cherry red border strips together. Measure the pieced top through the center from side to side; then cut two strips to this measurement. Pin and stitch them to the top and bottom of the quilt. Stitch the remaining cherry strips together. Measure the top through the center from top to bottom; then cut two strips to this measurement. Pin and stitch them to the quilt sides.

FINISHING

1 Using pearl cotton and a crewel needle (sharp point, large eye), stitch large decorative cross-stitches on the panels. Secure with small backstitches on the wrong side of the panels. Machine embroider at the ends of the two outer pink panels as desired (see quilt plan on page 66).

2 Measure the pieced top and trim the backing fleece to ½" larger all around. Spread the fleece backing right side down on a flat surface; then smooth the pieced top, right side up, on top. Baste together in a grid with safety pins or thread.

3 Using a walking foot and a straight stitch, quilt in the ditch around the main panels.

4 Quilt a decorative wave stitch along the royal blue sashing strips and in the royal blue border.

5 Add decorative stitches to the appliqué triangles as shown on the quilt plan.

6 On the outer cherry border, straight stitch four parallel rows at slightly wider intervals each time.

7 Stitch the binding strips with diagonal seams to make a continuous length to fit all around the quilt; bind the edges with a double-fold binding, mitered at the corners.

Alternative color schemes

1 Hot colors shine on a neutral background. **2** Bluish green and yellow produce a more masculine look. Batik fabrics were used for the appliqué. **3** A sophisticated scheme, reminiscent of a winter day with ice and snow. **4** Lime green and pink are perfect colors for a young girl, for a modern decor, or if you just like pink!

1
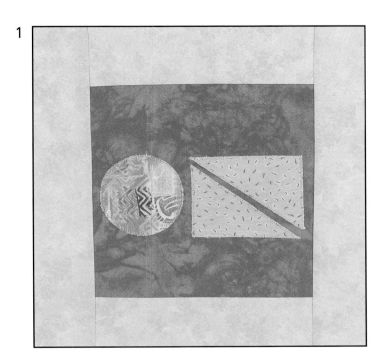

2

3
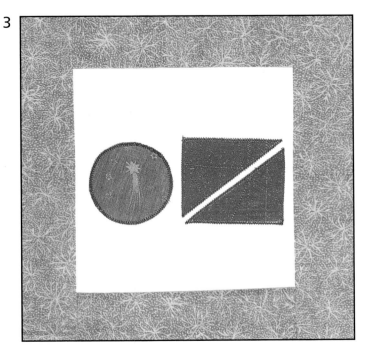

4
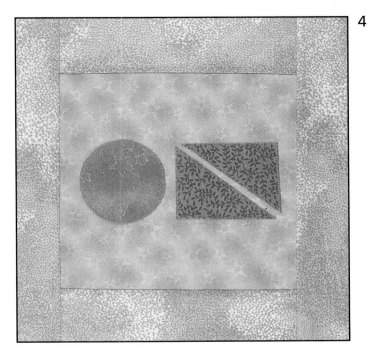

Tumbling Bows

DESIGNED BY

Dorothy Wood

Shadow appliqué is one of the quickest methods of appliqué. The pieces are simply sandwiched between a sheer fabric and the quilt top, and then stitched together by machine using a straight stitch. The fabrics appear paler underneath the sheer fabric, so bold colors work best for the appliqué pieces.

MATERIALS

All fabrics used in the quilt are 42" wide, 100% cotton, except the white fabric, which needs to be 54" or wider

Background and backing: 2¾ yards of white (bleached muslin)

Binding, border squares, and appliqués:
1 yard of striped fabric
1 fat quarter (18" x 22") each of pastel lilac, blue, and green
6" x 12" piece each of bold lilac, blue, and green

Quilt top: 1⅛ yards of sheer white fabric (voile or netting)

Batting: 48" x 56"

Fusible web: 18" x 24"

Pale green embroidery floss

Large piece of paper, at least 36" x 44"

CUTTING

1 From the white fabric, cut:
   1 rectangle, 36½" x 44½", for quilt top
   1 rectangle, 48" x 56", for backing

2 From the striped fabric, cut:
   22 squares, 4½" x 4½"
   5 binding strips, 2½" x 42"

3 From the pastel fabrics, cut:
   8 lilac squares, 4½" x 4½"
   7 blue squares, 4½" x 4½"
   7 green squares, 4½" x 4½"

4 Trace the triangle pattern on page 75 onto template plastic and cut out. Draw 32 triangles onto the smooth side of the fusible web in rows of four, allowing at least ¼" between the shapes. Cut out the shapes just outside the drawn lines.

Quilt plan

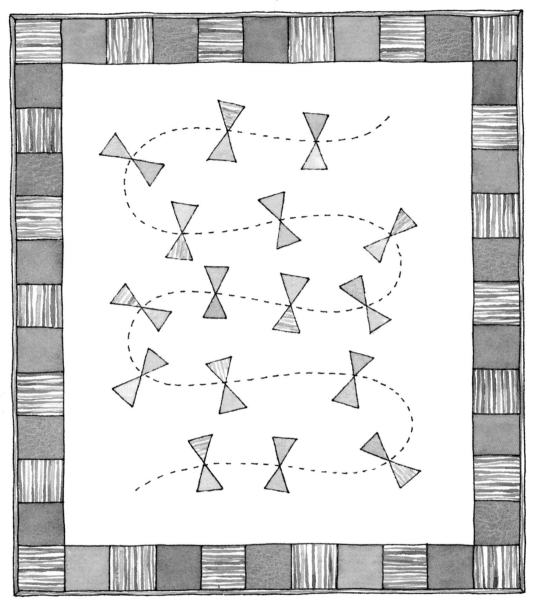

Finished size: 44" x 52"

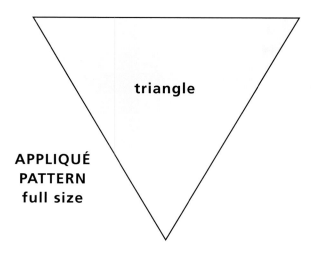

triangle

**APPLIQUÉ
PATTERN
full size**

ASSEMBLING THE QUILT TOP

1 Enlarge the quilt pattern shown in diagram 2. To do this, draw a 36" x 44" rectangle on a large piece of paper. Mark a grid of 4" squares on the rectangle. Then transfer the triangles onto the paper one square at a time using a pencil or fine-point permanent marker and the triangle template. Also transfer the curved line.

diagram 2

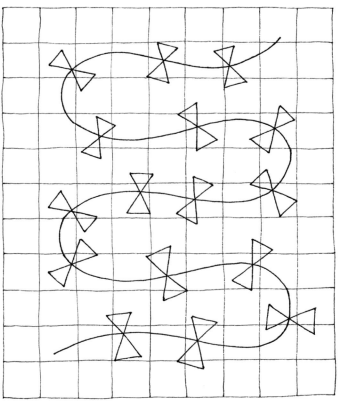

5 Press one set of four triangles onto each of the pastel fabrics, one set of four onto each of the bold fabrics, and two sets of four triangles on to the striped fabric, arranging the first set so that the stripes are horizontal and the second so that the lines are vertical (diagram 1). Cut out all triangles exactly on the marked lines.

diagram 1

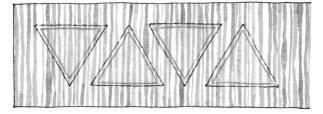

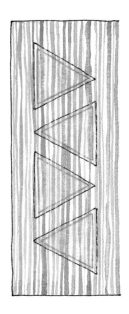

2 Pin the background fabric over the pattern and, using a pencil or quilt-marking pen, trace the design onto the fabric. You only need to mark a cross to indicate the position and direction of each bow.

3 Remove the papers from the fabric triangles and position them, right side up, on the background fabric following the pattern. Fuse in place with your iron.

4 Lay the sheer fabric on top of the right side of the appliqué quilt top and baste through the middle in both directions and around the outside edge.

ADDING THE BORDERS

1 Stitch the 22 striped squares and the 22 pastel squares together to make the borders, referring to the quilt plan on page 74 for color placement. The top and bottom of the quilt will require 9 squares each and each side border will require 13 squares. Use a ¼" seam allowance and press the seam allowances toward the darker colors (diagram 3).

diagram 3

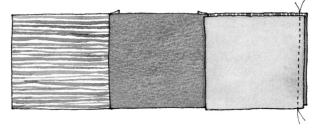

2 Pin the shorter strips to the top and bottom edges of the white center panel. Measure the border strips to make sure that they will fit exactly. If necessary, trim the center panel to fit; then stitch the top and bottom borders in place using a ¼" seam allowance. Press the seams toward the borders.

3 Pin the side borders in place, carefully matching the seams where they intersect with the top and bottom borders. Stitch and press as for the top and bottom borders.

FINISHING

1 Spread the backing right side down on a flat surface; then smooth out the batting and the

quilt top, right side up, on top. Pin about ½" from the ends of each bow (diagram 4). Baste along the marked curved line to hold the fabric in exactly the right place for the hand quilting.

2 Machine stitch around each bow, overlapping the stitching slightly where the ends meet (diagram 4).

diagram 4

3 Quilt in the ditch around the inner edge of the border. Machine stitch between each of the squares, backstitching at the inner edge to secure the threads. Trim all thread ends.

4 Using three strands of embroidery floss, work running stitches through all three layers along the marked curved line, referring to "Big-Stitch Quilting" on page 14. Begin and finish each length with small backstitches on the reverse side.

5 Join the binding strips with diagonal seams to make a continuous length to fit all around the quilt; bind the edges with a double-fold binding, mitered at the corners.

Alternative color schemes

1 Use pastel gingham fabrics and a baby print to make a crib quilt. 2 Choose a pretty print and pick out pale shades for the border and bold colors for the bows. 3 Make an even bolder quilt by using strong colors for both the border and the appliqué.
4 Contemporary print fabrics can make for an unusual and vibrant color scheme.

Hawaiian Snowflakes

DESIGNED BY

Sarah Wellfair

This quilt uses the Hawaiian appliqué technique where both the piece cut out and the background from which it was cut are used in the design—a clever and quick way of producing the nine snowflakes that make up this festive throw.

MATERIALS

All fabrics used in the quilt are 42" wide, 100% cotton

Snowflakes, outer borders, and binding:
1½ yards of purple

Blocks and inner borders:
1½ yards of cream

Backing: 2¾ yards

Batting: 48" x 48"

Fusible web: 1⅝ yards

CUTTING

1 From the purple fabric, cut:
2 strips, 10½" x 42"; crosscut into 5 squares, 10½" x 10½"
4 inner-border strips, 2½" x 42"
5 binding strips, 3" x 42"

2 From the cream fabric, cut:
3 strips, 10½" x 42"; crosscut into 10 squares, 10½" x 10½"
4 outer-border strips, 4½" x 42"

3 From the fusible web, cut:
5 squares, 10½" x 10½"*
*Use the snowflake pattern on page 82 to make a plastic template, and then trace around it onto the center of the smooth side of the fusible-web squares. Position these squares, glue side down, on the wrong side of the purple fabric squares and press to fuse.

4 Using small, sharp-pointed scissors, start cutting out the snowflake shape at one of the points of the snowflake (see note on page 81). Cut all around the shape to produce a background-snowflake shape and a snowflake shape; both will be used for the appliqué (see diagram 1). Make five of each.

diagram 1

Quilt plan

Finished size: 42½" x 42½"

NOTE

To make it easier to start cutting out the snowflake shapes, use pointed scissors and fold the shape in half, then make a small snip at one flake tip and insert the scissor points (diagram 2). Open out and continue cutting round the shape.

diagram 2

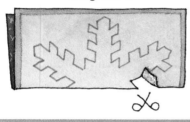

STITCHING

1 Remove the paper from the back of a purple snowflake and then position it, right side up, on top of a cream square, making sure that it is centered. Fuse the snowflake in place with your iron.

2 Remove the paper from the back of the corresponding purple background shape and position it, right side up, on top of another cream background square, aligning all raw edges. Press to fuse in place. Repeat with the remaining snowflakes and background-snowflake shapes to make nine blocks total. (The extra square can be set aside for machine-appliquéing practice.)

3 Stitch a narrow zigzag around the edges of the snowflakes. On the cream squares, appliqué the outer edges of the snowflake outline; on the purple squares, appliqué the inner edges of the snowflake outline.

4 Following the quilt plan on page 80, position the snowflake blocks, alternating cream and purple, and stitch them together in three

rows of three blocks each using a ¼" seam allowance. Join the rows. Press the seams toward the darker fabrics.

ADDING THE BORDERS

1 Measure the pieced top through the center from side to side, and then trim two of the 2½" purple border strips to this measurement. Pin and stitch them to the top and bottom of the quilt. Press the seams toward the borders.

2 Measure the pieced top through the center from top to bottom, and then trim the two remaining purple border strips to this measurement. Pin and stitch them to the quilt sides. Press the seam allowances toward the borders.

3 Repeat steps 1 and 2 using the 4½" cream outer-border strips. Press the seams toward the purple borders.

FINISHING

1 Piece the backing and then trim it and the batting 2" larger than the pieced top. Spread the backing right side down on a flat surface; then smooth out the batting and the pieced top, right side up, on top. Baste them together in a grid with safety pins or thread.

2 Free-motion quilt around the snowflakes, stitching on the cream fabric and using gold metallic thread and an 80/12 metallic needle. Quilt the cream borders in the pattern of your choice. Trim the excess batting and backing even with the edge of the borders.

3 Stitch the binding strips with diagonal seams to make a continuous length to fit all around the quilt; bind the edges with a double-fold binding, mitered at the corners.

APPLIQUÉ PATTERN
full size

snowflake

Alternative color schemes

1 Red and white make a striking combination. 2 Frosty blue and buttery yellow give a softer color scheme. 3 Dark blue with light blue and silver are dramatic and sparkling. 4 Christmas green and red make a really festive quilt.

Flowering Chains

DESIGNED BY

Janet Goddard

This cheery quilt is made from fabric scraps of many colors and patterns. It is constructed from two repeating blocks—a chain block and a simple appliquéd flower block. The layout of the quilt produces a secondary pattern of crossing lines.

MATERIALS

All fabrics used in the quilt are 42" wide, 100% cotton

Background squares: 2 yards of cream

Chain blocks, appliqué blocks, flower heads and centers: Fat quarters of at least 10 different print fabrics (or scraps totaling 2¼ yards. The minimum size for each scrap piece is 2½" square).

Appliqué:
¼ yard of green for stems and leaves

Borders and binding:
1⅜ yards of bright blue

Backing: 3¾ yards

Batting: 63" x 83"

Fusible web: 1¼ yards

CUTTING

1 For *each* of the 18 chain blocks, you will need five different print fabrics plus the cream background fabric.
For *one* chain block, cut the following:
Background fabric: 4 squares, 2½" x 2½"
Scrap fabric 1: 4 squares, 2½" x 2½"
Scrap fabric 2: 8 squares, 2½" x 2½"
Scrap fabric 3: 4 squares, 2½" x 2½"
Scrap fabric 4: 4 squares, 2½" x 2½"
Scrap fabric 5: 1 square, 2½" x 2½"

> ### NOTE
>
> Choose the fabrics for each block randomly rather than deliberating too carefully about whether the fabrics work together. As you can see from the quilt photo, the fabrics are stitched together in a riot of color.

2 For *each* of the 17 appliquéd blocks, cut:
Background fabric:
1 square, 6½" x 6½"
4 rectangles, 2½" x 6½"
Scrap fabric: 4 squares, 2½" x 2½"

Quilt plan

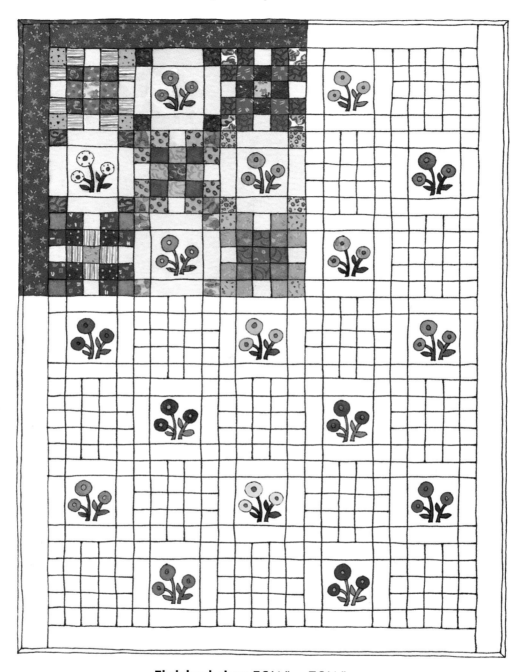

Finished size: 56½" x 76½"

3 From the bright blue fabric, cut:
   7 border strips, 3½" x 42"
   7 binding strips, 2½" x 42"

4 Use the patterns on page 87 to trace 17 sets of stems, leaves, flower heads, and flower centers onto the smooth side of the fusible

APPLIQUÉ PATTERNS
full size

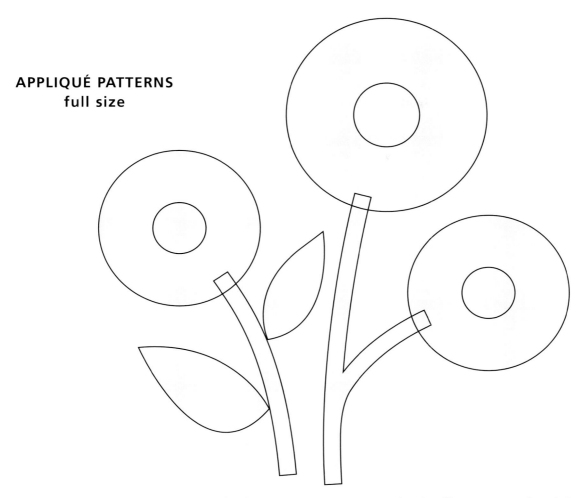

web. Cut out the shapes just outside the marked lines. Press the shapes for the stems and leaves to the wrong side of the green fabric, and the shapes for the flower heads and centers to the wrong side of the scrap fabrics.

5 Cut out the sets of appliqué shapes exactly on the marked lines on the fusible web.

STITCHING

Each chain block and appliqué block measures 10½" square, including seam allowances.

1 For the chain blocks, lay out the fabric squares in the order shown in diagram 1.

2 Stitch the squares together first in horizontal rows using a ¼" seam allowance. Press the

seams in the first row to the right; then stitch the second row and press the seams to the left. Repeat this for all rows. Stitch the rows together. Press.

3 Repeat to stitch 18 chain blocks total.

4 For the appliqué blocks, lay out the fabric pieces in the order shown in diagram 2.

diagram 1

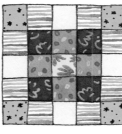

diagram 2

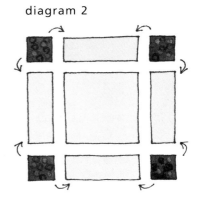

5 Stitch a 2½" scrap fabric square to each end of a background rectangle using a ¼" seam allowance. Press the seams toward the squares.

6 Stitch a background rectangle to each side of a 6½" background square. Press the seams toward the center.

7 Stitch the top and bottom rows to the center row. Press.

8 Remove the papers from the back of the stems, leaves, and flower pieces and position them in the center of each appliqué block (diagram 3). Press to fuse the fabrics in place and zigzag stitch around each shape, matching threads to fabrics. Make 17 blocks total.

diagram 3

9 Following the quilt plan on page 86, lay out the blocks in seven rows of five blocks, alternating chain and appliqué blocks. The first row begins with a chain block, the second row begins with an appliqué block, and so on.

10 Stitch the blocks together in horizontal rows. Press the seams in the first row to the right and the seams in the second row to the left. Press the seams alternately right or left for all rows.

11 Stitch the rows together and press the seam allowances all in one direction.

ADDING THE BORDERS

1 Stitch the seven border strips together into one long strip. Measure the pieced top through the center from side to side, and then cut two strips from the long strip to this measurement. Pin and stitch them to the top and bottom of the quilt.

2 Measure the pieced top through the center from top to bottom, and then cut two strips to this measurement. Pin and stitch them to the quilt sides.

FINISHING

1 Spread the backing, right side down, on a flat surface and smooth out the batting and the pieced top, right side up, on top. Baste together in a grid with safety pins or thread.

2 Use cream thread to quilt ½" from the seamline around each appliqué block, extending the quilting into the small background squares of the adjoining chain blocks (diagram 4).

diagram 4

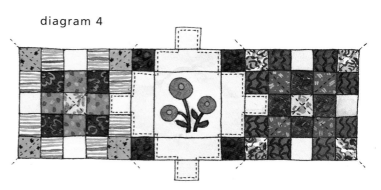

3 Use invisible thread to quilt on both diagonals through each chain block (diagram 4).

4 Stitch the binding strips with diagonal seams to make a continuous length to fit all around the quilt; bind the edges with a double-fold binding, mitered at the corners.

Alternative color schemes

1 and 3 These two blocks show the quilt stitched entirely in fabrics of a single color group, such as purples and lilacs. 2 and 4 These two blocks show the effect achieved with a dark background fabric.

Summer Garden

DESIGNED BY

Jane Coombes

I have always been attracted to the traditional Log Cabin block and its variations. This quilt is based on a variation called Courthouse Steps. I used just two rounds of steps in my blocks in order to create sufficient space for the appliqué. The theme of the appliqué designs is a summer garden: cottages, trees, flowers, and birds. The bright colors used also reflect summer; if you prefer more muted tones, you could choose autumnal colors and appliqué the flowers in yellow and brown to depict sunflowers and the coming of harvest time.

MATERIALS

All fabrics used in the quilt are 42" wide, 100% cotton

Center squares: ⅝ yard of light purple

Strips, appliqué, borders, and binding:
1½ yards of deep purple (main color)
1 yard of medium purple
⅞ yard of pink

Backing: 1¾ yards

Batting: 42" x 57"

Fusible web: ⅓ yard

Stabilizer: 1 yard of 12"-wide stabilizer

CUTTING

1 From the light purple fabric, cut:
3 strips, 4" x 42"; crosscut into 24 squares,
  4" x 4"

2 From the medium purple fabric, cut:
15 strips, 1½" x 42"; crosscut into:
  24 pieces, 1½" x 8"
  48 pieces, 1½" x 6"
  24 pieces, 1½" x 4"

3 From the pink fabric, cut:
15 strips, 1½" x 42"; crosscut into:
  24 pieces, 1½" x 8"
  48 pieces, 1½" x 6"
  24 pieces, 1½" x 4"

4 From the deep purple fabric, cut:
5 border strips, 4½" x 42"
5 binding strips, 2½" x 42"

NOTE

Stack each length strip of medium purple and pink into different piles on your work surface for methodical piecing.

Quilt plan

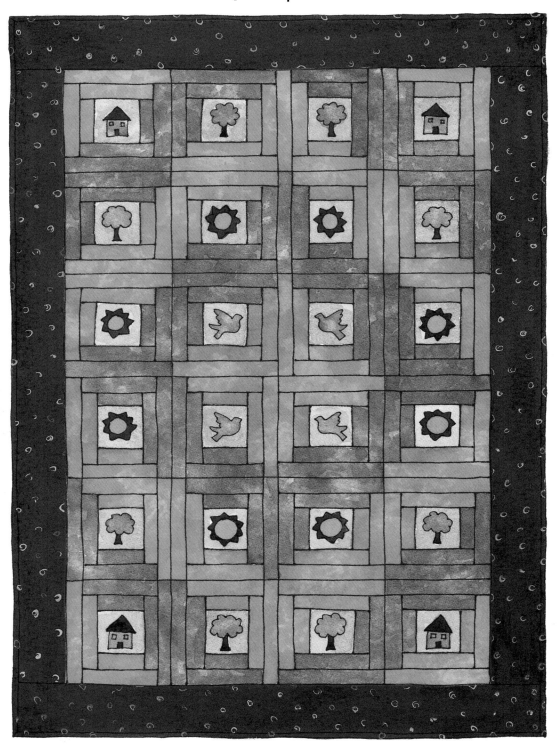

Finished size: 38" x 53"

5 For the appliqué shapes, trace the patterns on pages 94 and 95 onto the smooth side of the fusible web.

> **NOTE**
>
> For a professional finish, use the arrows on the templates to align the appliqué shape with the straight grain of the fabric.

6 For the birds, you will need two of each. Cut out the fusible-web shapes just outside the marked lines. Press the shapes to the wrong side of the remaining medium purple fabric.

7 For the flowers, you will need eight petal and eight center shapes. Cut out the fusible-web shapes outside the marked lines. Press the petal shapes to the wrong side of the deep purple fabric and press the center shapes to the pink fabric.

8 For the trees, trace eight trunks and eight foliage shapes. Cut out the fusible-web shapes outside the marked lines. Press the trunk shapes onto the deep purple fabric and press the foliage shapes onto the medium purple fabric.

9 For the cottages, trace four each of the door, roof, and wall shapes and eight of the window shapes. Cut out the fusible-web shapes outside the marked lines. Press the wall shapes onto the medium purple fabric, the roof and door shapes onto the deep purple fabric, and the window shapes onto the pink fabric.

10 Cut out all the appliqué shapes accurately following the marked lines on the fusible web.

STITCHING

1 Stitch a 4" medium purple strip to the top of a 4" light purple center square using a ¼" seam allowance (diagram 1a). Then stitch a 4" pink strip to the bottom of the square in the same manner (diagram 1b). Press the seams toward the strips.

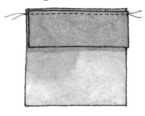
diagram 1a

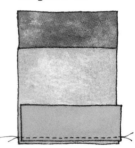
diagram 1b

2 Following diagram 2, add a 6" medium purple strip (3) and a 6" pink strip (4) to either side of the center square. Press the seam allowances toward the strips. Stitch another 6" medium purple strip (5) and another 6" pink strip (6) to the top and bottom of this unit. Press as before.

diagram 2
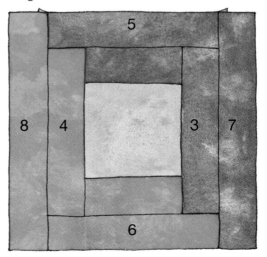

APPLIQUÉ PATTERNS
full size

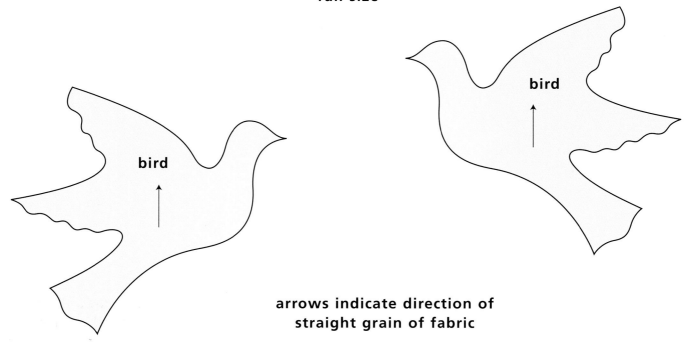

arrows indicate direction of
straight grain of fabric

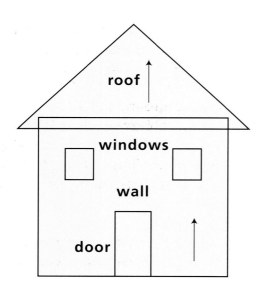

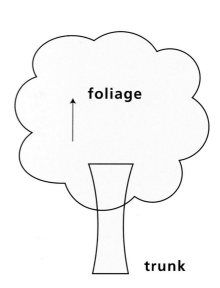

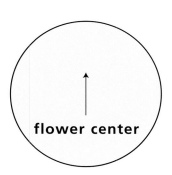

flower center

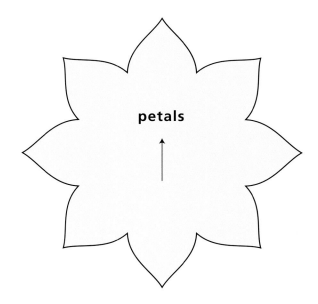

petals

and lay out the blocks in six rows of four blocks each, noting which way the longer seams are laid to achieve the secondary color sequence. Mark the top of each block with a pin to ensure that the appliqué is worked the right way up.

5 Remove the paper backing from the appliqué shapes and position each shape in its appropriate square. Press to fuse in place.

6 To stabilize the background before stitching, pin a 3" square of stabilizer (such as Stitch 'n Tear) to the wrong side of the block, covering the area behind the appliqué shape. Machine stitch in place using a zigzag, satin, or decorative stitch as desired.

3 Stitch an 8" medium purple strip (7) to one side of the block and an 8" pink strip (8) to the opposite side. Press as before. This completes one Courthouse Steps block. Repeat for the remaining 23 blocks.

4 To determine which shape to appliqué on each block, follow the quilt plan on page 92

7 Remove the stabilizer and press the block from the wrong side. Repeat for all blocks.

8 Reassemble the blocks following the quilt plan. Stitch the blocks together into six rows. Press the seams in opposite directions from one row to the next. This will assist accurate matching of seams when the rows are joined.

9 Pin and stitch the rows together to complete the pieced top, matching seams carefully. Press the seam allowances towards the bottom of the quilt.

ADDING THE BORDERS

1 Stitch three of the five deep purple border strips together end to end. Measure the pieced top through the center from top to bottom, and then cut two strips to this measurement from the joined strip. Stitch these borders to the sides of the quilt. Press the seams toward the borders.

2 Measure the pieced top through the center from side to side, and then trim the remaining two deep purple border strips to this measurement. Stitch them to the top and bottom of the quilt and press the seams as before.

FINISHING

1 Spread the backing, right side down, on a flat surface; then smooth out the batting and the pieced top, right side up, on top. Baste together in a grid with safety pins or thread.

2 Machine or hand quilt in the ditch around the blocks to emphasize the design of the patchwork. Use invisible thread on the top and a thread to match the backing fabric in the bobbin. Embellish the blocks by machine stitching a decorative embroidery stitch in curved lines first around the center pink cross shape, then around both the purple and pink diamond shapes. A curved border design can be machine stitched on the border if desired.

3 Join the binding strips with diagonal seams to make a continuous length to fit all around the quilt; bind the edges with a double-fold binding, mitered at the corners.

NOTE

Use a walking foot or even-feed foot on your sewing machine when stitching through three or more layers to prevent tucks on the underneath fabrics.

Alternative color schemes

1, 2, and 3 The original design is based on the use of light, medium, and dark shades of one color with a medium shade of a strong contrasting color. Here are three further examples using different colors. **4** Try using three primary colors plus green for a bright nursery quilt. *Note*: If time is short or you do not want to appliqué, simply use a novelty fabric for the block centers and select colors that complement it for the surrounding fabrics.

Appliqué Pinwheels

DESIGNED BY

Mary O'Riordan and Carol O'Riordan

This is a great beginner's project. The appliqué is simply a matter of tracing, pressing, and cutting out the curves, and the piecing couldn't be easier. Bright checks and fresh floral prints always look crisp on a muslin background, and the colored buttons add a whimsical touch.

MATERIALS

All fabrics used in the quilt are 42" wide, 100% cotton

Background fabric: 3⅛ yards of bleached muslin

Pinwheels: 1¼ yards total of bright prints and checks. (I used a different fabric for each pinwheel—25 in all, 8" square each—but you could use fewer fabrics and repeat the pinwheel colors.)

Fusible webbing: 3½ yards

Borders and binding: 1¼ yards of blue

Backing: 4 yards

Batting: 68" x 68"

25 assorted buttons

Template plastic

CUTTING

1 From the background fabric, cut:
17 strips, 6" x 42"; crosscut into 100 squares, 6" x 6"

2 Trace the pinwheel-blade pattern on page 101 onto template plastic. Cut out as accurately as possible. Use the plastic template to trace 100 pinwheel blades onto the smooth side of the fusible web. Cut out the shapes just outside the marked lines (diagram 1).

diagram 1

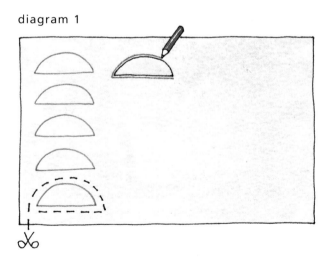

3 Press the fusible-web shapes to the wrong side of the bright print and checked fabrics. You need four of one color to make one pinwheel.

Quilt plan

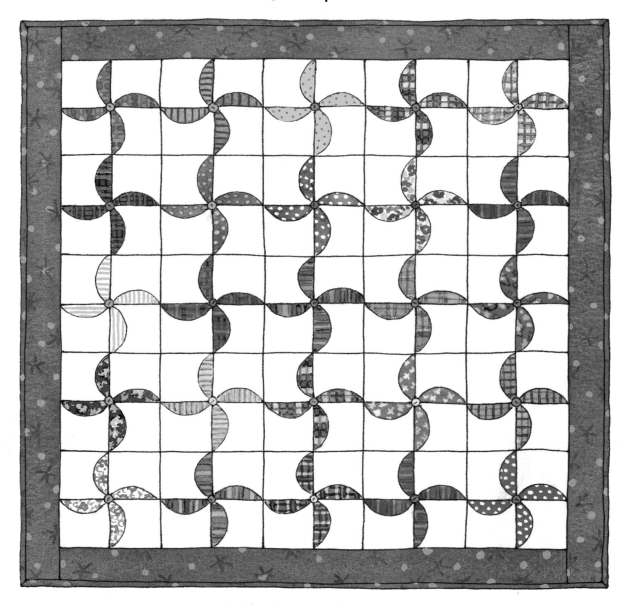

Finished size: 63½" x 63½"

APPLIQUÉ PATTERN
full size

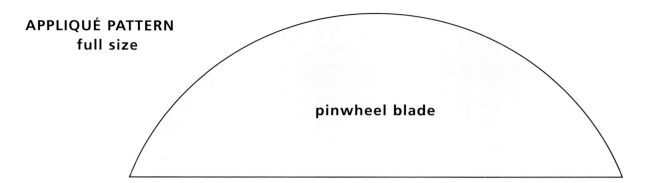

pinwheel blade

4 Cut out the pinwheel blades exactly on the marked lines on the fusible web.

5 From the blue fabric, cut:
6 border strips, 4½" x 42"
6 binding strips, 2" x 42"

STITCHING

1 Remove the papers from the back of the appliqués and position one pinwheel blade, right side up, on each background square (diagram 2). Press to fuse in place. Zigzag stitch along the curved edge of each blade.

diagram 2

2 Stitch four squares together using a ¼" seam allowance to make a Pinwheel block (diagram 3). Make 25 blocks.

diagram 3

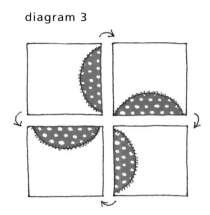

3 Following the quilt plan on page 100, pin and stitch the blocks into five rows of five blocks each. Pin and stitch the rows together, matching seams carefully, to complete the quilt top.

ADDING THE BORDERS

1 Stitch three of the 4½" blue border strips together. Measure the pieced top through the center from side to side, and then cut two strips to this measurement from the long strip. Pin and stitch the borders to the top and bottom of the quilt.

2 Stitch the remaining three 4½" blue border-strips together. Measure the pieced top through the center from top to bottom, and then cut two strips to this measurement from the long strip. Pin and stitch the borders to the quilt sides.

FINISHING

1 Spread the backing, right side down, on a flat surface; then smooth out the batting and the pieced top, right side up, on top. Baste together in a grid with safety pins or thread.

2 Beginning at the edge of the pieced block, machine or hand quilt in a continuous line, following the curves of the pinwheel blades all the way to the opposite edge. Rotate the quilt and return to the starting point along the center seams of the pieced blocks (diagram 4).

3 Use the plastic template to mark a pinwheel in each space where four blocks meet, and quilt these lines.

4 Stitch the binding strips with diagonal seams to make a continuous length to fit all around the quilt; bind the edges with a double-fold binding, mitered at the corners.

5 Stitch a button at the center of each block.

diagram 4

Alternative color schemes

1 Striped fabrics make a great background fabric, and by alternating the direction of the lines in each unit, the block has even more movement. **2** Because each pinwheel blade requires only a 2" x 6" rectangle of fabric, this quilt is a good way to use up lots of small scraps. **3** Make a romantic two-color quilt using a single favorite fabric for the pinwheels on a white or neutral background. **4** For a really vibrant quilt, choose bold fabrics for the background and the pinwheel blades, and use a different pair of fabrics for each block.

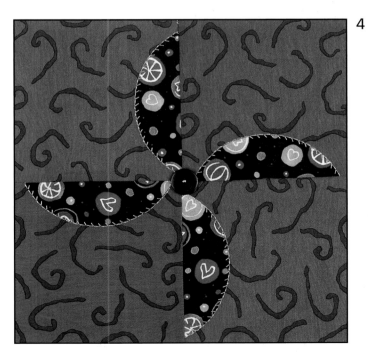

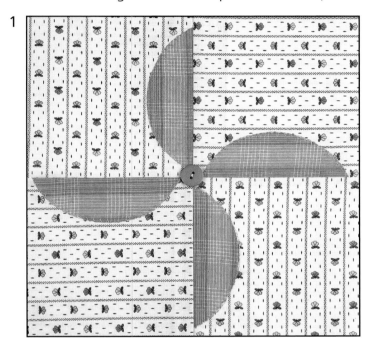

Blue-and-White Flowers

DESIGNED BY

Liz Lynch

This very simple quilt is an ideal project for lovers of handwork because it has virtually no piecing. The main section is divided into squares with quilting lines. Stylized blue-and-green flowers are appliquéd onto half the squares, while the remaining squares are quilted with a design that echoes the flowers. The quilting has been done by hand, although the straight lines could be machine quilted if desired.

MATERIALS

All fabrics used in the quilt are 42" wide, 100% cotton

Background fabric: 1 yard of white

Borders and flower petals: ¾ yard of pale blue floral

Corner blocks and flower petals: fat quarter (18" x 22") of dark blue floral

Flower leaves and stems: fat quarter of green

Backing: 1½ yards

Batting: 45" x 52"

Binding: ½ yard of blue

Template plastic

Card stock or one packet of 1"-long, 60° diamond paper pieces. (Quilt top requires 75 pieces.)

CUTTING

1 From the white fabric, cut:
1 rectangle, 34" x 42" (This will be cut down to size after the flowers have been appliquéd.)

2 From the pale blue fabric, cut:
2 border strips, 4½" x 33"
2 border strips, 4½" x 39½"
Reserve the remainder for the flower petals.

3 From the dark blue fabric, cut:
4 squares, 4½" x 4½"
Reserve the remainder for the flower petals.

APPLIQUÉ PATTERNS
full size

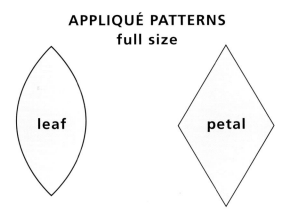

leaf

petal

Quilt plan

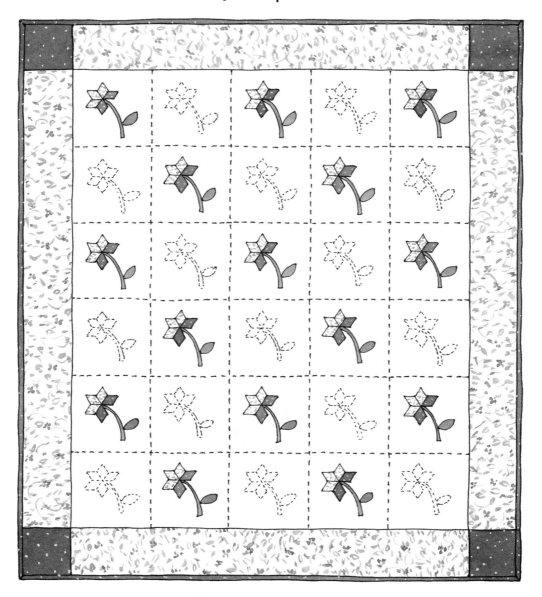

Finished size: 41" x 48"

diagram 1

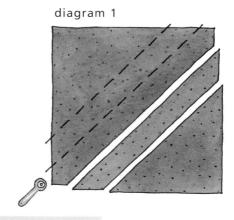

4 From the blue fabric, cut:
  4 binding strips, 2½" x 42"

5 From the green fabric, cut:
  3 bias stems, 1" wide, cutting across the diagonal at the longest point of the fabric (diagram 1). Reserve the remainder for the leaves.

6 To create the flowers and the leaves, use the patterns on page 105 to trace the leaf and petal shapes onto template plastic. Cut out as accurately as possible, and use them to make 75 paper petal templates and 15 paper leaf templates.

7 Using the plastic template, trace 45 petals onto the pale blue floral fabric, adding a ¼" seam allowance all around. Cut out on the marked seam-allowance line. Likewise, trace and cut 30 petals from the dark blue floral fabric. Cover the 75 paper templates with the fabric petals and baste to secure (diagram 2).

diagram 2

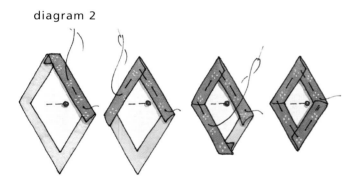

8 Use the leaf template to cut 15 leaves from the green fabric, adding a ¼" seam allowance around each shape. Cover the paper leaf shapes with the fabric and baste to secure (diagram 3).

diagram 3

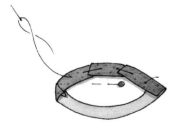

9 To make the stems, press each of the three 1" green bias strips in half lengthwise, wrong sides together. Crosscut the strips to make 15 stems, each 4" long.

STITCHING

1 Following the quilt plan opposite, prepare the quilt top by lightly marking the background fabric with a marking pencil in a grid of 6½" squares, five squares across and six down. These will be the final quilting lines. Center the grid, but note that any excess fabric around the edge of the grid can be trimmed away later.

2 Position one stem in a curve on the first square, leaving enough room for the flower to fit nicely into the block. Place the folded edge of the stem along the outer curve (diagram 4).

diagram 4

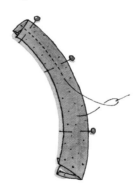

3 Pin and stitch lengthwise through the center of the stem with a fine backstitch in matching green thread. At the base of the stem, turn up a small seam allowance and stitch in place. Trim away the seam allowance close to the backstitch line, fold the stem over over along the stitching line, and appliqué stitch along the folded edge. Do not push the fabric over too firmly, but allow a little leeway to give the stem dimension.

4 To make each flower head, stitch five petal shapes together using two dark and three light blue fabrics (diagrams 5 and 6). Position them with the template papers still in place, making sure to cover the top raw edge of the stem. Pin and stitch using matching blue thread and the appliqué stitch. Finally, position a leaf as desired and stitch in place.

diagram 5   diagram 6

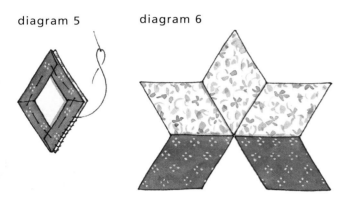

5 Remove all basting threads. From the back of the work, carefully cut away the background fabric to leave a ¼" seam allowance and remove the papers (diagram 7). If not torn, the papers can be stored for future use.

diagram 7

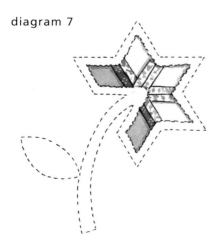

6 Place a 6½" square of template plastic on top of one appliquéd flower and, with a dark pen, mark an outline of the flower, leaf, and stem. Cut out. Use this as a template for the remaining blank squares to ensure all subsequent flowers are shaped exactly as the first one.

7 Repeat the appliqué process in the remaining 14 blocks, alternating every other block in the grid (see quilt plan).

8 Use the plastic template to mark the flower design quilting lines in the blank blocks.

ADDING THE BORDERS

1 Trim the center section, leaving a ¼" seam allowance all around outside of the grid.

2 Pin and stitch the two short border strips to the top and bottom edges of the quilt center. Press the seam allowances toward the borders.

3 Pin and stitch a dark blue corner square to one long border strip, right sides together. Press the seam allowances toward the square. Repeat on the other end. Pin and stitch the border to one long side of the quilt. Press the seam allowances toward the border. Repeat to add the remaining border strip to the other long side of the quilt.

FINISHING

1 Spread the backing right side down on a flat surface, and then smooth out the batting and the pieced top, right side up, on top. Baste together in a grid with safety pins or thread.

2 Hand quilt the appliquéd flowers closely around each shape, and quilt the replicated flower design in the blank squares. Machine or hand quilt the grid lines.

3 Stitch the binding strips with diagonal seams to make a continuous length to fit all around the quilt; bind the edges with a double-fold binding, mitered at the corners.

Alternative color schemes

1 Pink flowers would make a perfect quilt for a baby girl. **2** and **3** Primary colors give a striking, contemporary look for a toddler. **4** A striped background and white flowers take the quilt out of the nursery to create a lap quilt or table topper that would look lovely in any room, especially at Christmas.

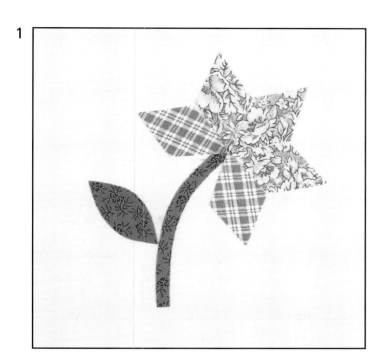

THE CONTRIBUTORS

Jane Coombes is a patchwork and quilting tutor and is a member of the teaching team at Creative Quilting near Hampton Court in Surrey.

Nikki Foley is an interior designer and uses this to her advantage when designing quilts and patterns for her business, the Sewing Shed: thesewingshed@aol.com

Janet Goddard writes patterns for magazines and books and teaches patchwork across Hertfordshire, Essex, and North London.

Liz Lynch teaches classes in patchwork quilting at her studio near Truro, Cornwall, and also at the Quilt Room in Dorking, Surrey.

Mary O'Riordan is an experienced quiltmaker who works at the Quilt Room in Dorking, Surrey.

Gail Smith opened her shop, Abigail Crafts, after completing a City and Guild course; she is a qualified adult education teacher, running local patchwork groups.

Sarah Wellfair is a qualified teacher who runs a full program of workshops from her patchwork shop, Goose Chase Quilting, at Leckhampton in Gloucestershire.

Alison Wood teaches classes and works part-time at the Quilt Room in Dorking, Surrey.

Dorothy Wood is an author and designer who has written and contributed to over 20 needlecraft books.

INDEX

New and Bestselling Titles from

Martingale ®
& COMPANY

America's Best-Loved Craft & Hobby Books®
America's Best-Loved Knitting Books®

That Patchwork Place®

America's Best-Loved Quilt Books®

NEW RELEASES

Alphabet Soup
Big Knitting
Big 'n Easy
Courtship Quilts
Crazy Eights
Creating Your Perfect Quilting Space
Crochet from the Heart
Fabulous Flowers
First Crochet
Fun and Funky Crochet
Joined at the Heart
Little Box of Knitted Ponchos and Wraps, The
Little Box of Knitted Throws, The
Merry Christmas Quilts
More Crocheted Aran Sweaters
Party Time!
Perfectly Brilliant Knits
Polka-Dot Kids' Quilts
Quilt Block Bonanza
Quilts from Grandmother's Garden
Raise the Roof
Saturday Sweaters
Save the Scraps
Seeing Stars
Sensational Knitted Socks
Sensational Sashiko
Strip-Pieced Quilts
Tea in the Garden
Treasury of Scrap Quilts, A

APPLIQUÉ

Appliqué Takes Wing
Easy Appliqué Samplers
Garden Party
Stitch and Split Appliqué
Sunbonnet Sue: All through the Year
WOW! Wool-on-Wool Folk-Art Quilts

LEARNING TO QUILT

101 Fabulous Rotary-Cut Quilts
Happy Endings, Revised Edition
Loving Stitches, Revised Edition
Magic of Quiltmaking, The
Quilter's Quick Reference Guide, The
Sensational Settings, Revised Edition
Your First Quilt Book (or it should be!)

PAPER PIECING

40 Bright and Bold Paper-Pieced Blocks
50 Fabulous Paper-Pieced Stars
300 Paper-Pieced Quilt Blocks
Easy Machine Paper Piecing
Fanciful Quilts to Paper Piece
Hooked on Triangles
Quilter's Ark, A

TOPICS IN QUILTMAKING

Basket Bonanza
Cottage-Style Quilts
Everyday Folk Art
Focus on Florals
Follow the Dots . . . to Dazzling Quilts
Log Cabin Quilts
More Biblical Quilt Blocks
Quilter's Home: Spring, The
Scatter Garden Quilts
Shortcut to Drunkard's Path, A
Strawberry Fair
Summertime Quilts
Tried and True
Warm Up to Wool

CRAFTS

Bag Boutique
Collage Cards
Creating with Paint
Painted Fabric Fun
Purely Primitive
Stamp in Color
Trashformations
Vintage Workshop, The: Gifts for All Occasions
Year of Cats...in Hats!, A

KNITTING & CROCHET

200 Knitted Blocks
365 Knitting Stitches a Year: Perpetual Calendar
Classic Crocheted Vests
Crocheted Socks!
Dazzling Knits
First Knits
Handknit Style
Knitted Throws and More for the Simply Beautiful Home
Knitting with Hand-Dyed Yarns
Little Box of Crocheted Hats and Scarves, The
Little Box of Scarves, The
Little Box of Scarves II, The
Little Box of Sweaters, The
Pleasures of Knitting, The
Pursenalities
Rainbow Knits for Kids
Sarah Dallas Knitting
Ultimate Knitted Tee, The

Our books are a\
at bookstores ar
favorite craft, f
and yarn retai
If you don't
the title you
looking for, visi
www.martingale-
or contact us

1-800-426-

International: 1-425-
Fax: 1-425-486-
Email: info@martinga

06/05